World Wisdom
The Library of Perennial Philosophy

The Library of Perennial Philosophy is dedicated to the exposition of the timeless Truth underlying the diverse religions. This Truth, often referred to as the *Sophia Perennis*—or Perennial Wisdom—finds its expression in the revealed Scriptures as well as the writings of the great sages and the artistic creations of the traditional worlds.

The Perennial Philosophy provides the intellectual principles capable of explaining both the formal contradictions and the underlying unity of the great religions.

Ranging from the writings of the great sages who have expressed the *Sophia Perennis* in the past, to the perennialist authors of our time, each series of our Library has a different focus. As a whole, they express the inner unanimity, transforming radiance, and irreplaceable values of the great spiritual traditions.

The Spirit of Indian Women appears as one of our selections in the Sacred Worlds series.

Sacred Worlds Series

The Sacred Worlds series blends images of visual beauty with focused selections from the writings of the great religions of the world, including both Scripture and the writings of the sages and saints. Books in the Sacred Worlds series may be based upon a particular religious tradition, or a theme of interest, such as prayer and virtue, which are found in all manifestations of the sacred.

Other Books by Judith and Michael Fitzgerald

Christian Spirit, World Wisdom, 2004
The Sermon of All Creation: Christians on Nature, World Wisdom, 2005
The Universal Spirit of Islam, World Wisdom (2006)
Indian Spirit: Expanded Edition, World Wisdom (2007)

Other Books by Michael Oren Fitzgerald

Yellowtail: Crow Medicine Man and Sun Dance Chief, University of Oklahoma
Press, 1991
Light on the Indian World: The Essential Writings of Charles Eastman (Ohiyesa),
World Wisdom, 2002
Indian Spirit, World Wisdom, 2003
Foundations of Christian Art, by Titus Burckhardt, edited by Michael Oren
Fitzgerald and Susana Marin, World Wisdom (2006)
The Sun Dance Way, World Wisdom (2006)
Introduction to Hindu Dharma: Discourses by the 68th Jagadguru of Kanchipuram,
World Wisdom (2007)

Films Produced by Michael Oren Fitzgerald

The Sun Dance Way, World Wisdom (2006)

CI

The Spirit of Indian Women

Edited by

Judith Fitzgerald
and
Michael Oren Fitzgerald

Introduction by

Janine Pease

www.worldwisdom.com

The Spirit of Indian Women
©2005 World Wisdom, Inc.

Design by Judith Fitzgerald

Library of Congress Cataloging-in-Publication Data

The Spirit of Indian women / edited by Judith Fitzgerald and Michael Oren Fitzgerald.
    p. cm. – (Sacred worlds series)
  Includes bibliographical references and index.
  ISBN-10: 0-941532-87-9 (pbk. : alk. paper)
  ISBN-13: 978-0-941532-87-7 (pbk. : alk. paper)
  1. Indian women–North America–History–19th century. 2. Indian
women–North America–Social conditions. 3. Indian women–North
America–Attitudes. I. Fitzgerald, Judith, 1951- II. Fitzgerald, Michael
Oren, 1949- III. Sacred worlds series (Bloomington, Ind.)

E98.W8S66 2005
305.48'897'009034–dc22

                                                                        2005007677

Printed on acid-free paper in China.

For information address World Wisdom, Inc.
P.O. Box 2682, Bloomington, Indiana 47402-2682

www.worldwisdom.com

Table of Contents

Preface

The Spirit of Indian Women provides a glimpse into the sacred world of the nomadic American Indian women of the nineteenth century. Photographs of women who actually lived the nomadic life combine with words of olden-day Indian leaders to present the feminine cultural ideal.[1] This book is an elegy for the women of this irreplaceable world, who were the perfect complement to the great chiefs and warriors. Indian women are sometimes thought of as subservient to the men, in part because of the very difficult circumstances that were imposed upon women in the early reservation era. The words of these olden-day leaders correct these mis-impressions and demonstrate the essential feminine role in their ancestral lifeway, with an emphasis on their traditional spirituality. Their own words and their own faces eloquently and poignantly communicate the wisdom, the strength, and the beauty of soul that characterized traditional American Indian women. While all of the American Indians presented here have passed from this earth, the heroic ideal that they represent stands as a model for all people.[2]

Many of these photographs have never before been published, so how have they been selected? Most of these photographs are taken from several thousand photographs that we have collected over the past thirty years. The majority of the photographs in our collection are the result of research in the Library of Congress in 1974. All of the photographs ever submitted for copyright protection are in that facility, and at that time it was still possible to roam freely through the stacks and to easily obtain copies of those photographs whose copyright protection had expired. We limited our selection of photographs to only women who were raised during the pre-reservation era.[3]

We are also grateful to include photographs from the collection of the late philosopher, Frithjof Schuon, compiled by him over a period of some fifty years. Although well known among scholars of comparative religion, many readers will not be familiar with Schuon. From his youth, Schuon had a profound and, what was to become, a lifelong interest in and affinity with the Plains Indians of North America.[4] In a career that spanned more than fifty years, Schuon wrote over twenty-five books that touched on diverse aspects of all the world's great religions, including that of the Plains Indians. He corresponded with many American Indian leaders and received photographs from many sources. For several of the photographs in the Schuon collection, the identity of both woman and photographer are unknown,[5] as they were gifts to Schuon and the information was not provided to him.

Our research on American Indian oratory and writings started in 1970 when Michael was the graduate teaching assistant in the course "Religious Traditions of the North American Indians" at Indiana University taught by Joseph Epes Brown.[6] It was through Dr. Brown that we met both Thomas and Susie Yellowtail and Benjamin Black Elk, the son of the revered Sioux holy man. From that time we both studied the American Indians, particularly the Plains Indians, and Michael continuously sought out the oratory and writings that concerned the spiritual traditions of the pre-reservation nomads.

The traditional world of the American Indians had no written language, so written documentation of this wisdom starts with the coming of the white man. This greatly limits the overall time period for the direct recording of the words of the pre-reservation American Indians.[7] In addition to the words of the nomadic elders, we have added selected writings from the generation taught directly by these traditional nomads. All of the education of the youth was through the oral teaching of the elders. This storytelling was the basis of the transmittal of the tribal wisdom from one generation to the next, or more precisely from the generation of the grandparents to the grandchildren, because the children spent countless hours under the tutelage of the grandparents while the parents provided for the material needs of the family. This process was an integral part of the children's education and in this way each third generation provided a vital link to the ancestral tribal traditions. Plains Indian youth born around the turn of the nineteenth century still had the benefit of an integral education directly from the "old timers," as many American Indians affectionately refer to the last generation that lived in the nomadic era of the Plains Indian culture. That generation is the last direct living link to the nomadic pre-reservation era, and most of them are no longer with us. While there is not a precise time that defines this generation, we have chosen to only include writings or oratory from the elders born before 1910.[8]

In order to present an accurate picture of the women's spirituality, we have divided the book into four distinct sections. The first section, entitled "The Role of Indian Women," presents both tribal statements and observations of male leaders about the role of women.[9] The next section, "Celestial Femininity," presents traditional tribal stories that illustrate the important role played by divine femininity in establishing their sacred culture.[10] The third section, "Intercessors with the Sacred," sets forth a few of the many tribal legends and history in which women were important intercessors who brought sacred teachings or sacred power to various tribes.[11] The last and largest section, "Women's Voices," presents the words of many esteemed women elders who have passed on to the "other side camp." An extensive annotated bibliography of autobiographies of American Indian women has been posted on the publisher's Internet site for further study.[12]

The women's traditional social role is as the owner and guardian of the home, including the education of all children until the age of eight or nine years. Women and grandparents are held in particularly high esteem because they are primarily responsible for safeguarding and transmitting the traditional spiritual values to the next generations. The women's focus on the home and the children is the perfect complement to traditional man's function of family protector in his role as hunter and warrior. We believe that these writings demonstrate that the social roles of men and the women were different, but complementary, and that every woman was the spiritual equal of her husband.

The Spirit of Indian Women introduces us to some of the foremost members of that tradition, in both photographs and words. We see the great emphasis the American Indians placed on moral character and their intimate contact with God's immeasurable, wild, and virgin Nature. It is evident that they strongly believe that the sacred spirit within every man and every woman is mysteriously linked to the Great Spirit, and that their collective vocation is to live in harmony with the teachings of the Great Spirit. Their entire culture was built upon these precepts. In today's technological world, we often lose our connection to anything of sacred value that can provide a balance for the disequilibriating factors that we encounter on a daily basis. It is our hope that the insights conveyed in *The Spirit of Indian Women* will help each of us to better understand the sacred spirit that dwells in every person.

Judith & Michael Oren Fitzgerald
Moose, Wyoming
July, 2004

notes

1. This book is a companion volume to *Indian Spirit* (see "Other Books by Judith and Michael Fitzgerald"), which presented photographs and words of only men as an elegy to the great chiefs, and in an attempt to provide a glimpse into the sacred world of the American Indian.

2. *The Spirit of Indian Women* contains wisdom from many American Indian tribes, but it has a certain focus on the Plains Indians because they were the last area to succumb to the white encroachment and thus their wisdom and their photographs are the best preserved of all American Indian tribes. When considering Plains Indian spirituality, it is evident that the many variations among the tribes are too vast and diverse to create a definitive statement about what it entails, but few would deny that there are unifying themes, including the sacred quality of virgin Nature, the use of the Sacred Pipe, and above all the idea of a Supreme Being. This book focuses on those common themes. As with other civilizations, it is evident that not all American Indians lived up to the cultural ideal, but that ideal is nevertheless a reality.

3. Photographic technology was not widely available until the second part of the nineteenth century, so there are few records of the nomadic tribes of the Eastern part of the United States. We have therefore chosen only photographs of Western tribes, who still lived in virgin Nature during the first years of photography.

4. Schuon was formally adopted into the family of Chief James Red Cloud—a grandson of the great Sioux chief well known to history—in 1959 at Pine Ridge, South Dakota, and given the Sioux name Brave Eagle, Wambli Ohitika. Years later, he was adopted into the family of Thomas Yellowtail, the Crow medicine man and Sun Dance chief, who was one of the most admired American Indian spiritual leaders of the last century. The story of Yellowtail's life is revealed in *Yellowtail: Crow Medicine Man and Sun Dance Chief*, recorded and edited by Michael Oren Fitzgerald, University of Oklahoma Press, 1991.

5. We are very grateful to Mike Cowdrey, one of the foremost experts on Native American photography, who painstakingly reviewed both *Indian Spirit* and this book and provided us with many missing names. Cowdrey corrected several errors in the recorded names of the women who appear on these pages.

6. Joseph Epes Brown recorded and edited Black Elk's story of the seven sacred rites of the Oglala Sioux in *The Sacred Pipe*, University of Oklahoma Press, 1951.

7. As *The Spirit of Indian Women* only focuses on their sacred heritage, we have not included statements about the interaction with the dominant white culture unless there is a comparison of the sacred or moral values of the two races.

8. This does not deny that much of the wisdom of these old timers has been preserved in later generations, but the later generations did not have the benefit of learning directly from those who actually lived the traditional life of complete freedom in virgin Nature. The further one travels from the source, the more difficult it is to know the authenticity of the recorded words, owing to a wide variety of factors. We have tried to select writings that stay as close as possible to the source of the ancestral wisdom.

9. On the social plane, the men often spoke for the family and tribal groups; thus, relatively few of the words recorded in the earliest encounters with white society were by women, including the early reservation period. The first section therefore includes a selected number of comments by men about the role of women, and some of the tribal folklore and history was also recorded from men.

10. Many of the American Indian legends and myths are extremely long, making it difficult to present them in a succinct fashion. In order to provide this overview, we have edited many of the myths, while maintaining the precise recorded words. We have tried to preserve the essential teachings, while realizing that simplifications lose some of the overall character of the entire narrative.

11. There are two distinct ways in which women were intercessors: for the tribe and for the individual or family. We have combined both of these groups within the same category, with a certain emphasis on stories that have a broader tribal impact.

12. We are indebted to Gretchen Bataille and Kathleen Mullen Sands for creating a bibliography that served as an initial foundation for our bibliography.

Introduction

It is an honor to introduce to you *The Spirit of Indian Women*. This volume brings to us a combination of images and voices from American Indian women. The historic and written voices of, and about, American Indian women are remarkably profound. By reading this book, we are privileged to hear the thoughts and words of Indian women along with the intense beauty of their images. This gift of voice and image affords us an opportunity to travel across time and cultures, to listen to, and to observe these beautiful mothers, grandmothers, and matriarchs, all of them Indian women. This gift counters the invisible, silent status ascribed to American Indian women by history and literature. American Indian women played significant roles in American Indian families, clans, communities, and nations. Their thoughts and words, in teachings, stories, songs, and ceremonies, and their countenance in beauty, strength, spirit, and dignity, made possible the very survival of American Indian people.

The Spirit of Indian Women is a research feat of major proportion, for the writings and therefore the voices of American Indian women are obscured by the weight of an enormously oppressive series of centuries in this country. And the search for images of quality and dignity, befitting American Indian women, was a task nearly as daunting as locating and identifying the writings, for photographers were intent on recording the "primitive," the romantic, the "vanishing Indian race." Our chance to hear and observe Indian women is dramatically enhanced by this collection of voices and images. We can glimpse the faces of American Indian women and their poignant words for a greater understanding of American Indian life. This is a book I plan to give to my sisters, my daughter, and my granddaughter, and I know it will go everywhere with me. *Aho!* Thanks to Michael and Judy Fitzgerald and World Wisdom Books; you have created an extraordinary gift of writings and images for the reader, *The Spirit of Indian Women*.

American Indian women are virtually ignored by the historians. Nineteenth century historians exclusively focused on men's leadership, men in military conflicts, and men as the heads of households, families, and communities. Theories of history's "famous man" or of the "man whose time has come" drive humanity's historical narratives. Beatrice Medicine, Lakota anthropologist and historian, comments about Indian women and history:

> I believe that women's activities and women's orientation to the Lakota
> lifestyles have been slighted. History is fashioned by events and relation-
> ships in the lives of both men and women, within a cultural milieu.[1]

Further, those traders and military men who maintained journals of their time with the Indians, lent a listening ear and observing eye to the Indian men. About visitors to the Hidatsa, Peters notes,

> When visitors approached an Indian village, they were met by a delegation of men in colorful and exotic costumes. Indian men assumed elaborate hairstyles, decorated robes, and military regalia. The men took charge of all ceremonies dealing with white visitors, especially those involving trade between other tribes and whites.[2]

The problem of hearing and seeing American Indian women was monumental. As history about the life and times of American Indians comes down to our generation, their omission damages historical works and leaves us with less than half the story.

American history has a propensity for following the events of conflict. Mention of American Indians nearly always connects with wars between the agents of the United States or the colonies, and American Indian nations. Historians' obsession with the themes of "American progress" and the "transformation" of North America eclipsed American Indian life from the scene, as they symbolized the antithesis to progress.[3] In "Problems in Indian History," Fred Hoxie comments:

> as for Native American history, it is remarkable that in the span of a century, Indians have gone from the forest primeval to a footnote, and Indian history has devolved from high adventure to demographic speculation.[4]

Progress, transformation, and struggles render American Indian women, in essence, invisible.

Let us talk about the challenge of hearing the voices of American Indian women. From our place in the twenty-first century, voices and faces from the past seem far away, in time and distance. What conditions put such distance between us and our precious American Indian grandmothers and great grandmothers? Historians, missionaries, teachers, and ethnographers who were there, were held captive by cultural biases that predisposed them to narratives, studies, observations, and images that were "conditioned by their own cultures and times. It never occurred to them to look beneath the surface of what they saw. And, what they saw was misleading."[5] Robert A. Trennert's research on the education of Indian girls and women, described the mid-nineteenth-century view held by Americans about Native Americans:

> Although recent scholarship has suggested that the division of labor be-

tween the sexes within Indian societies was rather equitable, mid-nine-teenth-century Americans accepted a vision of Native American women as slaves toiling endlessly for their selfish, slovenly husbands and fathers in an atmosphere of immorality, degradation, and lust.[6]

The degraded status of American Indian women was evidenced in curricular instructions from federal Indian Commissioner Morgan in 1900, when he said that "higher education in the sense ordinarily used has no place in the curriculum of Indian schools." Indian service school officials described Indians as incapable of learning, a "child race." Thus, domestic work was emphasized for the training of American Indian girls and women.

In spite of this highly prejudiced and misinformed view, there were Indian women who wrote about their lives, and photographers who captured their images with respect and dignity. From traditional American Indian culture, American Indian women knew the power of thought and the power of words. In *Literature of the American Indian*, A. Lavonne Brown Ruoff comments:

> As employed in religious rituals, thought and word can bring rain, heal physical and mental sickness, maintain good relations, bring victory against an enemy, win a loved one, or ward off evil spirits. Because of the great power of thought and word, Indian people feel both should be used with care.[7]

American Indian people have demonstrated their strong oral tradition through the tradition of creative writing. American Indians mastered the written word to preserve oral traditions, and to document tribal histories. In the nineteenth century, many American Indian authors wrote histories in the hope that their work would "remind whites of their tribes' long existence as peoples and convince them to respect the Indians rights to the land."[8] Speaking also included the power of silence, which N. Scott Momaday called "the dimension in which ordinary and extraordinary events take their proper places."[9]

The power of words was carried into the formal Indian oratory. Speeches were made to "inspire warriors or to celebrate a victory over an enemy. Most Indian orators were men. Plains Indians only occasionally allowed a female warrior or strong medicine woman to speak in public. Some women did become influential speakers."[10] The oratory was often placed in the context of major public rituals and ceremonies. Placed in that rich context, American Indian literature, thoughts, and words, were vested in ritual dramas, songs, narratives, and life histories.[11] The literary works have a particularly vital quality, in reenactments that require the broad participation of speakers, storytellers, dancers, singers, and audience. To render American Indian literature (dramas, songs, ceremonials, stories) as mere words isolates the words from the dynamic qualities of the literature in performance, like the whirring sound of birds' wings, the action of the dance steps, the evocative landscapes and homelands (against the rimrocks tinted rose in the setting sun), the camp sounds in the background, and meaningful declarations of dancers' regalia in color and symbolism.[12]

American Indian literature, both from the oral and written traditions, shows several dominant themes. First, is the belief that human beings "must be in harmony with the physical and spiritual universe. And, that such harmony may be achieved through the power of thought and the power of word."[13] A deep reverence for the land, sacredness of direction, the importance of the circle, and a strong sense of community are key themes in American Indian oral and written literature.[14] These themes are brilliantly represented here, in these writings.

Media images and stereotypic portrayals of American Indian women distort reality. Indian women rarely take any lead role in movies, or have lines that afford an Indian woman a voice. When you do see them up close, the conditions are deplorable, beyond pitiful. These images and portrayals are far from the actual roles and status of American Indian women. The forced removal of Indian nations to reservations, coupled with the loss of tribal economies dealt an enormous blow to all American Indian people. The struggle for homelands, sustaining virtual existence, prisoner of war experiences, conditions of reservation confinement, famine and disease, attacked American Indian families, with a decimating affect. Over several centuries, the diseases of smallpox, flu, and measles killed close to 90% of the American Indian people, who had numbered near five million in 1500. (The Crow population collapsed from 8,000 in 1600 to only 1,200 people in 1900.) The tumultuous changes and incumbent tragedies altered American Indian life, twisting and complicating role continuity.

American Indian women were remarkably resilient, in spite of these unimaginable frontal assaults on Indian people. Beatrice Medicine, Lakota anthropologist and historian, reflects that,

> Lakota women's roles as household provisioners have retained a certain stability. Women continue to maintain the house—to cook, clean, and care for children. Because of the socio-economic situation in most native communities, women are assuming a greater share as economic providers.[15]

Whether the times were changing or lands were lost, there were still children to raise. Child rearing was a primary and dominant role for American Indian women, assuming the entire control over the children until they were able to provide for themselves.[16] Among the Creek of the southeast, the girl's education continued under her mother and other clan women, including practical and moral instruction.[17]

As "primary socializers of children," American Indian women were the essential keepers of culture, language, worldview, rituals, and practices; in essence the purveyors of beliefs and behaviors.[18] Grandmothers were master teachers of history and culture as they told the tribe's myths and legends to their grandchildren, especially during the wintertime. Virginia Beavert, a Yakima Indian woman, collected her tribe's legends in *The Way It Was,*

> There were times when there was more than one storyteller involved, which made it a more interesting evening. Many questions were answered in the minds of the children; for instance why did the characters in the legend do things five times? It was explained that this was part of our lives, the parts of our bodies, the part of the religion, and many other things we take for granted in our everyday living.[19]

Ruoff also describes the role of the audience, namely to give gifts to the storytellers, and provide a feast as the storytelling concluded.[20] The rich tradition of signing among American Indian people further enhanced the telling with emphasis, action, even mimicry. Responses from the listeners were expected and elicited. Further, the grandmothers' stories were accompanied in the Crow tradition with a story-stick, a thirty inches long stick bedecked with miniature figures and objects that could be brought into the vivid Old Man Coyote or Red Woman stories. The nation's knowledge was held and taught by the women, the keepers of the people, the keepers of the culture.

American Indian creation stories contrast with the Judeo-Christian beliefs about where woman came from. Hoxie notes that,

> Crows did not believe that the creator made women after men or that women were derived from men. Instead all the versions of the tribal creation story that have been collected indicate that two genders were made at the same time and from the same materials.[21]

In further analysis of the Crow Indian mythology, Hoxie describes the spiritual status of females as "sharing equal, and autonomous status" that was comparable with their male counterparts' status.[22] For the Hidatsa of the upper Missouri River—the earth lodge people—the tribes' mythology and religious life reflected a "dependence on women, and their regenerative powers," being the origin of life.[23] Peters documents that,

> Women were in charge of the ritual blessing of each new earth lodge; they carried out annual rites before beginning to plant their gardens and in thanksgiving after the harvest; their White Buffalo Cow societies were often asked to perform a ceremony if the buffalo were too far away to hunt in safety, and they had an important role in "walking with the buffalo" in the men's buffalo calling ceremonies.[24]

The White Buffalo Cow societies' "walking with the buffalo" ceremony is an example of non-patriarchal religion, and derives from American Indian societies with a strong female presence within religious ceremonies. Among the Mandan, sacred bundles were owned and maintained by families, along matrilineal clan line, to the male heirs. The heir holding the bundle was obligated to prove his worthiness through giving feasts; a ceremony that could only be accomplished with support from the women in his family, and from his wives, who prepared food (that they had grown in huge gardens) and made appropriate gifts.[25]

The Lakota women play an integral part in the Lakota Sun Dance ceremony. Arthur Amiotte, in his article "The Lakota Sun Dance," narrates the instructions given to the four young women in the tree cutting ceremony:

> They are told of their significance and their relationship to the earth. They are told: "You are the pure, you are the good, you are the fecund, you are the new life of the people. Through you, the women, even the bravest of warriors must come into this earth.[26]

Sacred ceremonies of American Indian nations have essential roles played by women. In today's Lakota Sun Dance, a woman is selected to "become White Buffalo Calf Woman, she who will dance with the pipe and endure and sacrifice much the same way as the men do. One lady will attend to the ladies in the sweat lodge."[27] The Sun Dance ceremony follows a pattern of American Indian womens' significance in the sacred life of the Lakota people. Beatrice Medicine says, "it is a beautiful honor to be selected as a participant in any part of the Sun Dance. The Sacred Pipe Woman, the four virgins who cut the sacred tree, the people who do the work—all consider it an honor."[28] Women have honor and privilege in the spiritual life of the Lakota people.

In the Crow Indian tradition, as the eldest sister, I am called "little mother." My name is "Loves to Pray." This position is one of family responsibility, from my earliest assignments right up to the roles I carry out today. As a child and young woman, I held the responsibility for looking after my siblings and cousins. Elders tutored me in our tribal knowledge areas: in ceremony, dance, songs, traditions, and history. I aspired to be like my mother, my grandmothers, and my father's elder sister. Following their paths, it has been my honor to carry the sacred water into ceremonies, plan and prepare feasts and giveaways, conduct the sweat lodge ceremony, name children, sing love songs and lullabies, dance in the Dance of the Seasons, tell histories, and be the camp grandma. That I uphold these roles is evidence that my grandmothers fulfilled their roles as true Crow Indian women. In that respect, I am them. With First Maker's blessing, the circle will continue, with my daughter, "Leads the Parade Three Times," and my granddaughter, "Brave Heart."

JANINE PEASE
Crow/Hidatsa Indian Educator
22 February 2005

notes

1. Medicine, "*Indian Women and Traditional Religion,*" p. 161.
2. Peters, *Women of the Earth Lodges,* p. 161.
3. Hoxie, "*The Problems of Indian History,*" p. 35.
4. Ibid., p. 35.
5. Peters, *Women of the Earth Lodges,* pp. 161-162.
6. Trennart, "*Educating Indian Girls and Women,*" p. 380-381.
7. Ruoff, *Literatures of the American Indian,* p. 18.
8. Ibid., p. 74.
9. Ibid., p. 22.
10. Ibid., p. 61.
11. Ibid., p. 20.
12. Ibid., p. 23.
13. Ibid., p. 18.
14. Ibid., pp. 18-21.
15. Medicine, "*Indian Women and Traditional Religion,*" p. 171.
16. Spencer and Jennings, *Native Americans,* p. 426.
17. Ibid., p. 425.
18. Medicine, "*Indian Women and Traditional Religion,*" p. 170.
19. Quoted in Ruoff, *Literatures of the American Indian,* p. 40.
20. Ruoff, *Literatures of the American Indian,* p. 40.
21. Hoxie, *Parading Through History,* p. 191.

22. Ibid., p. 191.
23. Peters, *Women of the Earth Lodges*, p. 34.
24. Ibid., p. 40
25. Ibid., p. 36.
26. Amiotte, "*The Lakota Sun Dance*," p. 82.
27. Ibid., p. 76.
28. Medicine, "*Indian Women and Traditional Religion*," p. 168.

Bibliography

—Amiotte, Arthur. "The Lakota Sun Dance." *Sioux Indian Religion: Tradition and Innovation.* Norman: University of Oklahoma Press, 1987.

—Hoxie, Frederick. *Parading Through History: The Making of the Crow Nation in American, 1805-1935.* New York: Cambridge University Press, 1995.

—Hoxie, Frederick. "The Problems of Indian History." *Major Problems in American Indian History.* Lexington, MA: D.C. Heath and Company, 1994.

—Medicine, Beatrice (Lakota). "Indian Women and Traditional Religion." *Lakota Religion.* Norman: University of Oklahoma Press, 1987.

—Peters, Virginia Bergman. *Women of the Earth Lodges: Tribal Life on the Plains.* Norman: University of Oklahoma Press, 1996.

—Ruoff, A. Lavonne Brown. *Literatures of the American Indian.* New York: Chelsea House Publishers, 1991.

—Spencer, Robert F. & Jennings, Jesse D. *Native Americans.* New York: Harper and Row Publishers, 1965.

—Terrell, John Upton and Terrell, Donna M. *Indian Women of the Western Morning: Their Life in Early America.* New York: Anchor Books, 1976.

—Trennart, Robert A. "Educating Indian Girls and Women at Nonreservation Boarding Schools, 1878-1920." *Major Problems in American Indian History.* Lexington, MA: D.C. Heath and Company, 1994.

Unknown
Blackfeet

WHEN YOU SEE a new
trail, or a footprint you do
not know, follow it to the
point of knowing.

Uncheedah, grandmother of
Charles Eastman (Ohiyesa),
Wahpeton Dakota

PROBABLY THE AVERAGE white man still believes that the Indian woman of the old days was little more than a beast of burden to her husband. But the missionary who has lived among his people, the sympathetic observer of their everyday life, holds a very different opinion. You may generally see the mother and her babe folded close in one shawl, indicating the real and most important business of her existence. Without the child, life is but a hollow play, and all Indians pity the couple who are unable to obey the primary command, the first law of real happiness.

She has always been the silent but telling power behind life's activities, and at the same time shared equally with her mate the arduous duties of primitive society. Possessed of true feminine dignity and modesty, she was expected to be his equal in physical endurance and skill, but his superior in spiritual insight. She was looked to for the endowment of her child with nature's gifts and powers.

She was the spiritual teacher of the child, as well as its tender nurse, and she brought its developing soul before the "Great Mystery" as soon as she was aware of its coming. When she had finished her work, at the age of five to eight years, she turned her boy over to his father for manly training, and to the grandparents for traditional instruction, but the girl child remained under her close and thoughtful supervision. She preserved man from soul-killing materialism by herself owning what few possessions they had, and thus branding possession as feminine. The movable home was hers, with all its belongings, and she ruled there unquestioned. She was, in fact, the moral salvation of the race; all virtue was entrusted to her, and her position was recognized by all. It was held in all gentleness and discretion, under the rule that no woman could talk much or loudly until she became a grandmother.

The Indian woman suffered greatly during the transition period of civilization, when men were demoralized by whiskey, and possession became masculine. The division of labor did not readily adjust itself to the change, so that her burdens were multiplied while her influence decreased. Tribe after tribe underwent the catastrophe of a disorganized and disunited family life.

Charles Eastman (Ohiyesa), Wahpeton Dakota

Pretty Nose
Northern Cheyenne

Unknown
Nez Perce

THE WOMAN OF the household had no "lord and master" when it came to deciding where she and her children were to live.

In the home there came into being the faith and simplicity that marked the native people. There took root their virtues and cultural attributes. Forces, sensed but not seen, called good, went into the deep consciousness of these young minds, planted there by the Indian mother who taught her boy honesty, fearlessness, and duty, and her girl industry, loyalty, and fidelity. Into the character of babes and children mother-strength left the essence of strong manhood and womanhood. Every son was taught to be generous to the point of sacrifice, truthful no matter what the cost, and brave to the point of death. These impulses — generosity, truthfulness, and bravery — may be dressed and polished in schools and universities, but their fundamental nature is never touched.

After childhood days, mothers still could not forsake the part of guide and teacher — for youth, as well as childhood, must be directed, and there was no substitute. So Lakota mothers taught youth how to worship and pray, how to know mercy and kindness, and how to seek right and justice.

Luther Standing Bear
Oglala Lakota

THE WOMEN OF every clan of the Five Nations shall have a Council Fire ever burning in readiness for a council of the clan. When in their opinion it seems necessary for the interest of the people they shall hold a council and their decisions and recommendations shall be introduced before the Council of the Lords by the War Chief for its consideration.

From the Constitution of the Iroquois Nations

Unknown
Lakota

GRANDMOTHER, NEXT TO mother, was the most important person in the home. Her place, in fact, could be filled by no one else. It has been told and written that old people among the Indians were sacrificed when they became useless. If this is the case with other tribes, I do not know of it, but I do know that it was never done among the Lakotas. Most old people were revered for their knowledge, and were never considered worthless members to be got rid of. Parental devotion was very strong and the old were objects of care and devotion to the last. They were never given cause to feel useless and unwanted, for there were duties performed only by the old and because it was a rigidly-kept custom for the young to treat their elders with respect. Grandmother filled a place that mother did not fill, and the older she got the more, it seemed, we children depended upon her for attention. I can never forget one of my grandmothers, mother's mother, and what wonderful care she took of me. As a storyteller, she was a delight not only to me but to other little folks of the village. Her sense of humor was keen and she laughed as readily as we....Then grandmother, with the help of grandfather, was our teacher. When grandfather sang his songs, she encouraged us to dance to them. She beat time with him and showed us how to step with his tunes. Seldom did she go walking in the woods or on the plains without taking us with her, and these hours were profitable ones in knowledge, for scarcely was a word or an act not filled with the wisdom of life.

Luther Standing Bear
Oglala Lakota

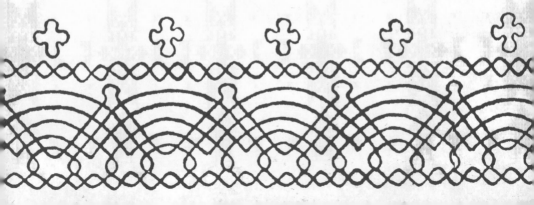

IN HIS WEAVING, painting, and embroidery of beads and quills the red man has shown a marked color sense, and his blending of brilliant hues is subtle and Oriental in effect. The women did most of this work and displayed vast ingenuity in the selection of native materials and dyes. A variety of beautiful grasses, roots, and barks are used for baskets by the different tribes, and some even used gorgeous feathers for extra ornamentation. Each was perfectly adapted in style, size, and form to its intended use.

This native skill combined with love of the work and perfect sincerity—the qualities which still make the Indian woman's blanket or basket or bowl or moccasins of the old type so highly prized—are among the precious things lost or sacrificed to the advance of an alien civilization. Cheap machine-made garments and utensils, without beauty or durability, have crowded out the old; and where the women still ply their ancient trade, they do it now for money, not for love, and in most cases use modern materials and patterns, even imported yarns and "diamond dyes"! Genuine curios or antiques are already becoming very rare, except in museums, and sometimes command fabulous prices.

Charles Eastman (Ohiyesa), Wahpeton Dakota

IT HAS BEEN said that the position of woman is the test of civilization, and that of our women was secure. In them was vested our standard of morals and the purity of our blood. The wife did not take the name of her husband nor enter his clan, and the children belonged to the clan of the mother. All of the family property was held by her, descent was traced in the maternal line, and the honor of the house was in her hands. Modesty was her chief adornment; hence the younger women were usually silent and retiring: but a woman who had attained to ripeness of years and wisdom, or who had displayed notable courage in some emergency, was sometimes invited to a seat in the council.

Thus she ruled undisputed within her own domain, and was to us a tower of moral and spiritual strength.

Charles Eastman (Ohiyesa), Wahpeton Dakota

Lizzie Bear Foot
Oglala Lakota

Holds the Pipe
Kiowa

TO KEEP THE young men and young women strictly to their honor, there were observed among us, within my own recollection, certain annual ceremonies of a semi-religious nature. One of the most impressive of these was the sacred "Feast of Virgins," which, when given for the first time, was equivalent to the public announcement of a young girl's arrival at a marriageable age.

The coming event was considered next to the Sun Dance in public importance. It always took place in midsummer, when a number of different clans were gathered together for the summer festivities, and was held in the center of the great circular encampment.

Here two circles were described, one within the other, about a ruddy heart-shaped rock which was touched with red paint, and upon either side of the rock there were thrust into the ground a knife and two arrows. The inner circle was for the maidens, and the outer one for their grandmothers or chaperones. Upon the outskirts of the feast there was a great public gathering, in which order was kept by certain warriors of highest reputation. Any man among the spectators might approach and challenge any young woman whom he knew to be unworthy; if the accuser failed to prove his charge, the warriors were accustomed to punish him severely.

Each girl in turn approached the sacred rock and laid her hand upon it with all solemnity. This was her religious declaration of her virginity, her vow to remain pure until her marriage. If she should ever violate the maidens' oath, then welcome that keen knife and those sharp arrows!

Our maidens were ambitious to attend a number of these feasts before marriage, and it sometimes happened that a girl was compelled to give one, on account of gossip about her conduct. Then it was in the nature of a challenge to the scandal-mongers to prove their words!

Charles Eastman (Ohiyesa), Wahpeton Dakota

PEOPLE WILL SAY that a woman who is having her moon should stay away from the ceremonies because she could ruin them, but they don't understand or know why this is. It is because a woman is the only one who can bring a child into this world. It is the most sacred and powerful of all mysteries. Certainly the man must be there to plant the seed, but his part is simple and relatively unimportant.

Some people focus on the Sun Dance and the male power of the sky, but it is to bless Mother Earth with new life that the dance is held. When we pray in the sweat lodge or in our ceremonies, we always remember <u>Maka Ina</u> [Mother Earth]. We get our health from Mother Earth and the herbs that grow from her. We use some for food and others for doctoring.

When a woman is having her time, her blood is flowing, and this blood is full of the mysterious powers that are related to childbearing. At this time she is particularly powerful. To bring a child into this world is the most powerful thing in creation. A man's power is nothing compared to this, and he can do nothing compared to it. We respect that power.

If a woman should come into contact with the things that a man prays with [pipe, rattles, medicine objects] during this time it will drain all the male powers away from them. You see, a woman's power and a man's are opposites — not in a bad way, but in a good way. Because of the power a woman has during this time it is best that, out of respect for her men and for their medicine things, she stay away from them. In the past they would build a little lodge for her, and their other female relatives would serve on her needs. She would get a rest from all her chores. It was not a negative thing like people think now. So you see, we did this out of our respect for this great mystery, out of respect for the special powers of women.

Joseph Rockboy
Yankton/Sicangu Dakota

Unknown
Lakota

AS SOON AS the wife realized that she was to become a mother, she withdrew from the society of her husband, though at all times he had her in his care. But the husband immediately found duties that occupied his time—the hunt, the war-party, or ceremonies. With the knowledge that a child was about to be born the thought of the couple was for its welfare, and both father and mother were willing to sacrifice for the sake of the health of the child and mother. Not till a child was five or six years of age did the parents allow themselves another offspring. As a consequence Lakota families were not large, four or five children being the rule. But disabled mothers were a rarity and many a grandmother was as strong as her granddaughter. And with all the demands placed by parenthood, seldom was the relationship between husband and wife weakened.

Luther Standing Bear, Oglala Lakota

IT IS THE mothers, not the warriors, who create a people and guide their destiny.

Luther Standing Bear, Oglala Lakota

The lineal descent of the people of the Five Nations shall run in the female line. Women shall be considered the progenitors of the Nation. They shall own the land and the soil. Men and women shall follow the status of the mother.

The women heirs of the Confederated Lordship titles shall be called Royaneh (Noble) for all time to come.

When a Lord holds a conference in his home, his wife, if she wishes, may prepare the food for the Union Lords who assemble with him. This is an honorable right which she may exercise and an expression of her esteem.

The Royaneh women, heirs of the Lordship titles, shall, should it be necessary, correct and admonish the holders of their titles.

From the Constitution of the Iroquois Nations

Unknown woman & child
Lakota

Blackfeet women

CONCERNING FIDELITY, HUMAN frailty must be taken into consideration, but the Indian woman was a true wife and the Indian man a true husband. The vows on both sides were taken seriously and both man and woman looked upon their marriage contract as something extremely vital to their position in the tribe. The integrity of the home was revered, and a man known as a good husband and a woman known as a good wife were honored members of society. Polygamy was never extensively practiced among the Lakotas, comparatively few men—chiefs or men of special note—taking more than one wife. But this arrangement was not assigned to divine instruction nor given a religious hue; it was wholly and solely an adjustment with the social plans of the tribe. A chief would have considered it much more dishonorable to have one overworked wife than to have two or three to share the duties of his household, and the women were of the same opinion. But fidelity was another Indian virtue to become weakened by the disruption of his society, for the white man was wont to take the things that pleased him.

Luther Standing Bear
Oglala Lakota

Ear of Corn
Miniconjou Lakota

AT THE FUNERAL of a chief woman, say: "Now we become reconciled as you start away. You were once a chief woman in the Five Nations' Confederacy. You once were a mother of the nations. Now we release you for it is true that it is no longer possible for us to walk about together on the earth. Now, therefore, we lay it (the body) here. Here we lay it away. Now then we say to you, 'Persevere onward to the place where the Creator dwells in peace. Let not the things of the earth hinder you. Let nothing that transpired while you lived hinder you. Looking after your family was a sacred duty and you were faithful. You were one of the many joint heirs of the Lordship titles. Feastings were yours and you had pleasant occasions . . .'"

From the Constitution of the Iroquois Nations

THE WOMEN ... MADE buffalo-corrals. Their lodges were fine....They tanned the buffalo-hides, those were their robes. They would cut meat in slices.... Their lodges all fine inside. And their things were just as fine.... Now, the men...were very poor. They made corrals. They had no lodges, they wore raw-hides...for robes. They wore the gamble-joint of the buffalo for moccasins. They did not know how they should make lodges. They did not know how they should tan the buffalo-hides. They did not know too, how they should cut dried meat, how they should sew their clothes. The women's chief told them: Over there near the corral are the men sitting in sight. All these women were cutting meat. Their chief did not take off the clothes she was wearing while cutting the meat. They were told by her: I shall go up there first, I shall take my choice. When I come back, you will go up one by one. Now we will take husbands. Then she started up. Then she went up to all those men. She asked them: Which is your chief? The men said: This one here, Wolf-robe [Napi]. She told him: Now we will take you for husbands. And then she walked to that Wolf-robe. She caught him. Then she started to pull him up. Then he pulled back. Then she let him loose. He did not like her clothes. While the other women were picking out their husbands, the chief of the women put on her best costume. When she came out, she looked very fine, and, as soon as Old Man saw her, he thought, Oh! there is the chief of the women. I wish to be her husband.

Story of the first marriage, told by Joseph Tatsey, Blackfeet

Many Horses (daughter of Sitting Bull), with son
Hunkpapa Lakota

WAMPUM STRINGS SHALL be given to each of the female families in which the Lordship titles are vested. The right of bestowing the title shall be hereditary in the family of the females legally possessing the bunch of shell strings and the strings shall be the token that the females of the family have the proprietary right to the Lordship title for all time to come.

If at any time it shall be manifest that a Confederate Lord has not in mind the welfare of the people or disobeys the rules of this Great Law ... the War Chiefs shall then divest the erring Lord of his title by order of the women in whom the titleship is vested. When the Lord is deposed the women shall notify the Confederate Lords through their War Chief. The women will then select another of their sons as a candidate and the Lords shall elect him. When a Lord is to be deposed, his War Chief shall address him as follows: "So you, __ __, disregard and set at naught the warnings of your women relatives. So you fling the warnings over your shoulder to cast them behind you.

"Behold the brightness of the Sun and in the brightness of the Sun's light I depose you of your title and remove the sacred emblem of your Lordship title. I remove from your brow the deer's antlers, which was the emblem of your position and token of your nobility. I now depose you and return the antlers to the women whose heritage they are."

The War Chief shall now address the women of the deposed Lord and say: "Mothers, as I have now deposed your Lord, I now return to you the emblem and the title of Lordship, therefore repossess them."

From the Constitution of the Iroquois Nations

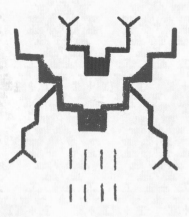

Unknown
Lakotas

Hattie Tom
Apache

EVEN TO THIS day the (sacred) pipe is very <u>Wakan</u>. Long ago a people were camping and two young men from the camp were going ahead, it is said. They were going along a ridge. Then suddenly a very beautiful woman appeared climbing the hill. She was coming, carrying something. So they stood watching her, it is said. Then one of the young men said, "Well, my friend, I will do it with her."

"Look, my friend, see clearly! She is not a woman, probably something <u>Wakan</u>," the other said. But the young man was not afraid.... So he went there but no further, for from the sky a very big cloud fell on them, it is said. And when it cleared away, the young man was nothing but bones lying there, it is said.

The woman-who-was-not-a-woman was coming in a <u>Wakan</u> manner....

So the other young man stood there trembling, it is said. Then the woman said this: "Young man, do not fear me!... I am bringing home news. I am bringing something so the people will live; it is the Buffalo Calf Pipe. They will live in a <u>Wakan</u> manner. I will assist all of the people by showing them good ways." She left saying, "Now after a while, I will arrive bringing news."

So the young man hurried home with the news, it is said. And then the crier took it and since the camp circle was large, the crier walked all around proclaiming the news, it is said. "Howo! Something is coming but it is coming in a <u>Wakan</u> manner so no one think anything evil. Follow good ways. In a very <u>Wakan</u> manner it comes," the crier proclaimed, it is said. And so all the people prepared themselves, it is said.

Now the woman came among the tipis, it is said. And she told them she had something, it is said. "The Buffalo Calf Pipe arrives here," she said, it is said. Anyone who does bad deeds and uses this pipe will be rubbed out," she said, it is said. The woman was a very beautiful woman, it is said. She was completely naked, it is said. Her hair was very long, it is said.

Thomas Tyon, Oglala Lakota

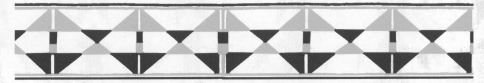

I WILL HERE relate the manner in which corn first came. According to tradition, handed down to our people, a beautiful woman was seen to descend from the clouds, and alight upon the earth, by two of our ancestors, who had killed a deer and were sitting by a fire roasting a part of it to eat. They were astonished at seeing her, and concluded that she must be hungry, and had smelt the meat—and immediately went to her, taking with them a piece of the roasted venison. They presented it to her, and she ate—and told them to return to the spot where she was sitting at the end of one year, and they would find a reward for their kindness and generosity.

She then ascended to the clouds, and disappeared. The two men returned to their village, and explained to the nation what they had seen, done, and heard.... When the period arrived for them to visit this consecrated ground, where they were to find a reward for their attention to the beautiful woman of the clouds, they went with a large party, and found, where her right hand had rested on the ground, corn growing—and where the left hand had rested, beans—and immediately where she had been seated, tobacco.

The first two have, ever since, been cultivated by our people as our principal provisions—and the last used for smoking. The white people have since found out the latter and seem to relish it as much as we do.

We thank the Great Spirit for all the benefits He has conferred upon us. For myself, I never take a drink of water from a spring, without being mindful of His goodness.

Black Hawk, Sauk

White Hawk (wife of Big Foot)
Miniconjou Lakota

Unknown
Hidatsa

AS I LAY sleeping, as I lay dreaming, out of the distance came one advancing, one whom I ne'er had seen before, but when her voice addressed me, straightway I knew her—Lo! 'Twas our Mother, she whom we know. I rose from sleeping, my dream remembering; Her words I pondered, words of our Mother. Then I asked of each one I met, Tell me, how far may Her shrine be? When I found it sweet smoke I offered unto our Mother.

Song for Mother Corn, Pawnee

"O, <u>WAKAN</u> <u>TANKA</u>, Grandfather, behold us! We are about to offer the pipe to You!" [Then holding the tobacco to the earth]:"O, You, Grandmother, upon whom the generations of the people have walked, may White Buffalo Cow Woman appear and her generations walk upon you in a sacred manner in the winters to come. O, Mother Earth, who gives forth fruit, and who is as a mother to the generations, this young virgin who is here today will be purified and made sacred; may she be like You, and may her children and her children's children walk the sacred path in a holy manner. Help us, O, Grandmother and Mother, with Your red and blue days!"

From the rite "Preparing a Girl for Womanhood," Black Elk, Oglala Lakota

ONCE, MANY GENERATIONS ago, there lived a beautiful goddess of the ocean – the "Woman of the White Shells," younger sister of the Moon. This goddess was the special patroness of beauty and grace and she imparted an attractiveness almost equaling her own to those into whose hearts she deigned to breathe. So that she would not be defiled, she lived in a cave.

One day when some maidens were passing near the mountain, suddenly the beautiful goddess appeared to them, sitting high up in the rocks, dressed in sparkling white cotton garments. She beckoned to the maidens to approach her, reassuring them with her friendly smile.

"Sit ye down by my side," she said to them, "and I will teach you the arts of women." Then with a sharp-edged fragment of jasper, she chipped out a mealing stone of lava. Next she fashioned another stone of finer rock, long enough to reach entirely across the mealing stone. Taking white shells and white kernels of corn, the goddess ground them together between the stones, demonstrating to her pupils a grace of movement before unknown to women. Now, leaning ever so lightly on her grinding stone and glancing slyly under her waving side-locks, she talked to the watching maidens, teaching them how to tease their lovers; then dashing the hair from her eyes, she turned back to the mealing trough and began to grind, singing meanwhile, in time with her labors, the songs that ever since young women have loved to sing, and young men loved yet more to listen to.

She stopped then and picked some long stems of grass which she made into a brush and used to sweep together the flour she had been grinding. Of this she gave to each of the maidens an equal measure.

"Take it," she said, "and remember how I have made it that ye may be blessed with children and make more for them and they for theirs. With it men and women shall cast their prayers to the Beloved and maidens shall beautify their persons." Then she took a little of the flour between her palms and applied it lightly to her face and bosom until her countenance appeared almost as white as her mantle and as smooth as dressed doeskin. And ever since that time women have won the most lingering of lovers with the wiles of the mealstone.

Zuni legend

A MAN WAS roaming over the prairie. He came to a place where people had camped and there he heard a woman crying. The man went to the place where the crying came from, but there was no one there, and he did not know what to think. When he went home he lay down, and in the night he had a dream. He dreamed that he saw a woman. The woman spoke to him and said: "I stay where the crying came from, and I was glad that you hunted me and tried to find me. I am going to help you to find me, and also let you see me. As soon as the sun goes down and it becomes a little dark, I want you to go to the place where you heard the crying. I will be there, and there you shall see me and I will tell you some things that you do not know."

When the man awoke he thought of the woman he was to see that evening, and so he watched and looked over the country until the sun went down. As soon as the sun disappeared and it became a little dark he went to the place where he had heard the crying. As soon as he arrived at this place, instead of hearing the crying he saw a woman. The woman spoke to the man and said: "Look, look at me, for I am the one who was crying at this place." The man looked at the woman and he saw that she was a fine-looking woman. She said again: "Young man, when the people passed over this place while hunting buffalo they dropped me. I have been crying ever since."... Then the woman said: "Look upon the ground where my feet rest." The man looked and there he saw a kernel of corn. This kernel of corn was speckled. "Now," said the woman, "pick up this kernel of corn and keep me always with you. My spirit is of Mother Evening Star, who gives us the milk that is in the corn. The people eat of us and have life. The women give the same milk from their breast. Keep me in your quiver and my spirit will always be with you."

The man took the kernel up and the woman disappeared. The man went home and kept the kernel close to him all the time.... He put the kernel of corn into a bundle and the bundle became a sacred bundle.... The young man became a great warrior. The Corn Woman spoke to him in a dream and said: "You must tell

(CONTINUED)

Unknown
Bannock

Unknown
Apsaroke

your mother to place me in a large hill of earth. When a stalk grows from the hill and you find corn upon the stalk do not eat it, but lay it away. Then the next spring tell your mother to plant some more corn and the next fall there will be a good crop and you will see how the corn has multiplied." The young man did as he was told. As the spring came the mother placed the kernel in a big hill of earth. And a stalk grew out of this hill with many kernels upon it. These she laid away until the next spring. Then she planted much more corn.

About that time the young man married. The young man and his wife had many children, and their children had children. When Corn Woman disappeared she told the man to tell his people, when they were ready to plant corn, to pray first to Mother Corn and then to Mother Earth. "When you have placed the corn in the earth then stand to the west and pray to Mother Evening Star to send rain upon the earth so that the corn will grow. Pray also to Mother Moon, who helps give life to people, and she will listen to what people say. Never drop a kernel upon the ground, for Mother Corn will curse you and your life will be shortened." Corn Woman also told the young man that when the cornfields were high, all the people were to take their children into the fields and to pass their hands over the stalks and then over the children. Thus the children would grow, and bad diseases would go away from them. Corn Woman also said: "When the tassels are out, then watch. There will be singing in the fields. Know that that singing comes from the sacred ear of the corn. Take it from the stalk, and take it to the old man, who will place it in the sacred bundle so that people will know that Mother Corn did sing to her people." The Pawnee worship Mother Corn because she represents Mother Evening Star.

The Corn Spirit, Skidi Pawnee

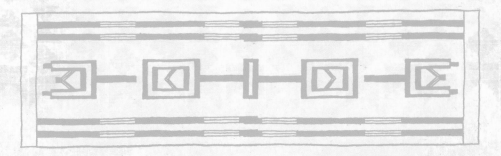

LONG AGO, WHEN Kloskurbeh, the great teacher, lived in the land, and there were as yet no other men, there came to him one day at noon a youth who said: "I was born of the foam of the waters; for the wind blew, and the waves quickened into foam, and the sun shone on the foam and warmed it, and the warmth made life, and that life is I. See, I am young and swift, and I have come to abide with you and be your help in all things."

Again on a day at noon there came a maiden and stood before the two and called them "my children," and the maiden said: "I have come to abide with you, and I have brought with me love. I will give it to you, and if you will love me and grant my wish, all the world will love me well, even the very beasts. Strength is mine, and I give it to whosoever may get me; comfort also; for though I am young my strength shall be felt over all the earth. I was born of the beautiful plant of the earth; for the dew fell on the leaf, and the sun warmed the dew, and the warmth was life, and that life is I."

Then Kloskurbeh lifted up his hands towards the sun and he praised the Great Spirit, and afterwards the young man and the young maid were man and wife, and she became the first mother. Kloskurbeh taught their children and did great works for them and when his works were finished he went away to live in the Northland until it should be time for him to come again. But the People increased until they were very many, and there came a famine among them; and then the first mother grew more and more sorrowful. Every day at noon she left her husband's lodge and stayed from him until the shadows were long. And her husband that dearly loved her was sad because of her sorrow.

The husband bade her come out and look at the beautiful sun. And while they stood side by side, there came seven little children that stood in front of them and looked into the woman's face, saying, "We are hungry. Where is the food?" Then the woman's tears ran down, and she said, "Be quiet, little ones; in seven moons you shall be filled, and shall hunger no more."

The husband reached out his hand and wiped away her tears and said, "My wife, what can I do to make you happy?" And she answered, "Take my life."

"I cannot take your life," said the man; "will nothing else make you happy?" (CONTINUED)

Unknown
Klamath

Wife of White Elk
Northern Cheyenne

"Nothing else," she answered. "Nothing else will make me happy." Then the husband went away to the Northland to take counsel with Kloskurbeh, and with the rising of the seventh sun he came again and said, "O, wife, Kloskurbeh has told me to do the thing you wish." Then the woman was glad and said: "When you have slain me, let two men lay hold of my hair and draw my body all around a field, and when they have come to the middle of the field, there let them bury my bones. Then they must come away; but when seven moons have passed let them go again to the field and gather all that they find, and eat; it is my flesh; but you must save a part of it to put in the ground again. My bones you cannot eat, but you may burn them, and the smoke will bring peace to you and to your children."

On the morrow when the sun was rising the man slew his wife and did as she had bidden. But when seven moons had gone by, and the husband came again to that place, he saw it all filled with beautiful tall plants; and he tasted the fruit of the plants and found it sweet, and he called it "Skarmu-nal," corn. And on the place where her bones were buried he saw a plant with broad leaves, bitter to the taste, and he called it "Utar-mur-wa-yeh," tobacco.

Then the people were glad in their hearts, and they came to his harvest; but when it was all gathered in, the man did not know how they should divide it, and he sent to Kloskurbeh for counsel.

When Kloskurbeh came and saw the great harvest, he gave thanks to the Great Spirit and said, "Now have the first words of the first mother come to pass, for she said she was born of the leaf of the beautiful plant, and that her power should be felt over the whole world, and that all men should love her. And now that she is gone into this substance, take care that this, the second seed of the first mother, be always with you, for it is her flesh. Her bones also have been given for your good; burn them, and the smoke will bring freshness to the mind. And since these things came from the goodness of a woman's heart, see that you hold her always in memory; remember her when you eat, remember her when the smoke of her bones rises before you. And because you are all brothers, divide among you her flesh and her bones—let all shares be alike—for so will the love of the first mother have been fulfilled."

Mrs. Joseph Nicolar, Penobscot

MOTHER CORN, WHO led our spirits over the path we are now to travel, leads us again as we walk, in our bodies, over the land…. She led our fathers and she leads us now, because she was born of Mother Earth and knows all places and all people, and because she has on her the sign (the blue-paint symbol) of having been up to Tirawahut, where power was given her over all creatures.

Prayer of the Mother Corn ritual, Pawnee

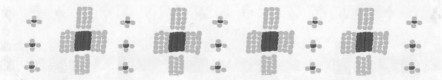

THE NEXT SONG is about a man to whom Mother Corn came in a dream; it happened very long ago. The song and the story are very old and have come down to us from our fathers, who knew this ceremony. Mother Corn spoke to this man in his dream. We are not told what she said to him, but when he awoke he started out to find the man in whose keeping was a shrine containing the ear of corn. As he walked he met a man and asked him, "Is it far to the lodge where the corn is?" The man pointed to a lodge some distance off and said, "It is within." Then the man who had had the dream walked toward the place. As he entered the lodge he saw a shrine hanging on one of the poles and he asked the keeper if it contained the sacred ear of corn, and he was told that it did. Then he took his pipe and offered smoke and prayer in the presence of the corn; because Mother Corn had appeared to him in a dream and had spoken to him he came to offer her reverence.

Kurahus [priest], speaking about Mother Corn, Pawnee

Family of Running Owl
Blackfeet

Wife of Man on the Hill
Miniconjou Lakota

I COME TO White Painted Woman,
By means of long life I come to her.
I come to her by means of her blessing,
I come to her by means of her good fortune,
I come to her by means of all her different fruits.
By means of the long life she bestows, I come to her.
By means of this holy truth she goes about.

I am about to sing this song of yours,
The song of long life.
Sun, I stand here on the earth with your song,
Moon, I have come in with your song.

White Painted Woman's power emerges,
Her power for sleep.
White Painted Woman carries this girl;
She carries her through long life,
She carries her to good fortune,
She carries her to old age,
She bears her to peaceful sleep.

You have started out on the good earth;
You have started out with good moccasins;
With moccasin strings of the rainbow, you have started out.
With moccasin strings of the sun's ray, you have started out.
In the midst of plenty you have started out.

Song for girls' puberty rites, Chiricahua Apache

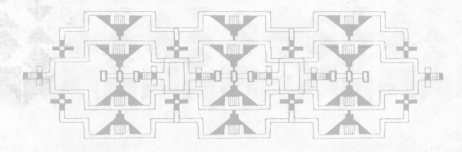

WHITE BUFFALO WOMAN'S words to the women: "My dear sisters, the women: You have a hard life to live in this world, yet without you this life would not be what it is. Wakan Tanka intends that you shall bear much sorrow—comfort others in time of sorrow. By your hands the family moves. You have been given the knowledge of making clothing and of feeding the family. Wakan Tanka is with you in your sorrows and joins you in your grief. He has given you the great gift of kindness toward every living creature on earth. You he has chosen to have a feeling for the dead who are gone. He knows that you remember the dead longer than do the men. He knows that you love your children dearly."

Retold by Lone Man, Teton Lakota

WHITE BUFFALO WOMAN'S words to the men: "Now my dear brothers: In giving you this pipe you are expected to use it for nothing but good purposes. The tribe as a whole shall depend upon it for their necessary needs. You realize that all your necessities of life come from the earth below, the sky above, and the four winds. Whenever you do anything wrong against these elements they will always take some revenge upon you. You should reverence them. Offer sacrifices through this pipe. When you are in need of buffalo meat, smoke this pipe and ask for what you need and it shall be granted you. On you it depends to be a strong help to the women in the raising of children. Share the women's sorrow. Wakan Tanka smiles on the man who has a kind feeling for a woman, because the woman is weak. Take this pipe, and offer it to Wakan Tanka daily. Be good and kind to the little children."

Retold by Lone Man, Teton Lakota

WHEN CHANGING WOMAN gets to be a certain old age, she goes walking toward the east. After a while she sees herself in the distance looking like a young girl walking toward her. They both walk until they come together and after that there is only one. She is like a young girl again.

Apache

Mollie Holds the Weasel
Absaroke

Unknown
Kiowa

THE TWO DIVINE SISTERS, Changing Woman and White Shell Woman, were left on the mountain alone.

The women remained here four nights; on the fourth morning, Changing Woman said: "Younger sister, why should we remain here? Let us go to yonder high point and look around us." They went to the highest point of the mountain, and when they had been there several days, Changing Woman said: "It is lonely here; we have no one to speak to but ourselves; we see nothing but that which rolls over our heads (the sun), and that which drops below us (a small dripping waterfall). I wonder if they can be people. I shall stay here and wait for the one in the morning, while you go down among the rocks and seek the other."

In the morning Changing Woman found a bare, flat rock and lay on it with her feet to the east, and the rising sun shone upon her. White Shell Woman went down where the dripping waters descended and allowed them to fall upon her. At noon the women met again on the mountain top and Changing Woman said to her sister: "It is sad to be so lonesome. How can we make people so that we may have others of our kind to talk to?" White Shell Woman answered: "Think, Elder Sister; perhaps some day you may plan how this is to be done."

Four days after this conversation, White Shell Woman said: "Elder Sister, I feel something strange moving within me; what can it be?" Changing Woman answered: "It is a child. It was for this that you lay under the waterfall. I feel, too, the motions of a child within me. It was for this that I let the sun shine upon me." Soon after the voice of the Talking God was heard four times, as usual, and after the last call He and Water Sprinkler appeared. They came to prepare the women for their approaching delivery.

In four days they felt the commencing throes of labor, and one said to the other: "I think my child is coming." She had scarcely spoken when the voice of the approaching god was heard, and soon the Talking God and Water Sprinkler were seen approaching. The former was the birthing assistant of Changing Woman, and the latter of White Shell Woman. To one woman a drag-rope of rainbow was given, to the other a drag-rope of sunbeam, and on these they pulled when in pain, as the Navaho woman now pulls on the rope. Changing Woman's child was born first. The Talking God took it aside and washed it. He was glad, and laughed and made ironical motions, as if he were cutting the baby in slices and throwing the slices away. They made for the children two baby-baskets, both alike; the foot-rests and the back battens were made of sunbeam, the hoods of rainbow, the side-strings of sheer lightning, and the lacing strips of zigzag lightning. One child they covered with the black cloud, and the other with the female rain.

Navajo legend about the birth of their tribe

Unknown
Oglala Lakota

THE BLOOD INDIANS have had medicine pipes for a very long time. There is one pipe among them that is so old that no one has any recollection of having heard of its being made by any one. So this pipe must be the real one handed down by the Thunder, for all medicine pipes came from the Thunder.

Once there was a girl who never could marry, because her parents could not find any one good enough for her. One day she heard the Thunder roll. "Well," she said, "I will marry him." Not long after this she went out with her mother to gather wood. When they were ready to go home, the girl's pack strap broke. She tied it together and started, but it broke again. Her mother became impatient; and when the strap broke the third time, she said, "I will not wait for you!" The girl started after her mother, but the strap broke again. While she was tying it together, a handsome young man in fine dress stepped out of the brush and said, "I want you to go away with me." The girl said, "Why do you talk to me that way? I never had anything to do with you." "You said you would marry me," he answered, "and now I have come for you." The girl began to cry, and said, "Then you must be the Thunder."

Then he told the girl to shut her eyes and not look, and she did so. After a while he told her to look, and she found herself upon a high mountain. There was a lodge there. She went in. There were many seats around the side, but only two people—an old man and woman. When the girl was seated, the old man said, "That person smells bad." The old woman scolded him, saying that he should not speak thus of his daughter-in-law. Then the old man said, "I will look at her." When he looked up, the lightning flashed about the girl, but did not hurt her. Because of this, the old man knew she belonged to the family. At night

(CONTINUED)

all the family came in one by one. The Thunder then made a smudge with sweet-pine needles, one at the door of the lodge, and one just back of the fire. Then he taught his wife how to bring in the bundle that hung outside. This was the medicine pipe. After a time Thunder's wife gave birth to a boy, later to another boy.

One evening the Thunder asked her if she ever thought of her father and mother. She said that she did. Then he asked would she like to see them. She said, "Yes." So he said, "Tonight we will go. You may tell them that I shall send them my pipe, that they may live long." When the time came, he told the woman to close her eyes, and once more she was standing near the lodge of her people. It was dark. She went in and sat down by her mother. After awhile she said to her mother, "Do you know me?" "No," was the answer. "I am your daughter. I married the Thunder." The mother at once called in all of their relations. They came and sat around the lodge. The woman told them that she could not stay long as she must go back to her lodge and her children, but that the Thunder would give them his pipe. In four days she would come back with it. Then she went out of the lodge and disappeared.

In four days the Thunder came with the woman, her two boys, and the pipe. Then the ceremony of transferring the pipe took place. When it was finished, the Thunder said that he was going away, but that he would return in the spring, and that tobacco and berries should be saved for him and prayed over. Then he took the youngest boy and went out. A cloud rolled away, and as it went the people heard one loud thunder and one faint one [the boy]. Now, when the Thunder threatens, the people often say, "For the sake of your youngest child," and the Thunder heeds their prayers.

When the Thunder left the woman and elder child behind, he said that if dogs ever attempted to bite them, they would disappear. One day a dog rushed into the lodge and snapped at the boy, after which nothing was seen of him or his mother, and to this day the owner of a medicine pipe is afraid of dogs.

Origin of the medicine pipe, Blood

Unknown
Warm Springs (Oregon)

Freckled Face
Southern Arapaho

THE FIRST PEOPLE, those are the ones that found the buffalo rock. Nearly starved were all the people. A man said to his wife, "Get some wood and build a fire." Then she arose, saying, "I shall go after firewood." She came to a place where there was wood, and, standing beside it, picked it up slowly. Then she heard singing and looked around. At last she saw it. On the cut-bank's side she sat down. The thing doing the singing was the buffalo rock. The earth was sliding down: that is how she came to see it. While it was singing, the rock said:

"Take me,
I am powerful."

On buffalo hair it was sitting for a bed. It stretched out its arms. In order that food might be obtained is the reason she saw it. She took it up, wrapped it in the hair and put it inside her dress. Now she knew some food would be obtained. She went back to the camp. She went to her husband's lodge. She went inside. She said to her elder sister, "Tell our husband that I shall make medicine." So the elder one said to him, "My younger sister is about to make medicine." He said, "I have faith. Let her make medicine that we may have food." Then he called out, inviting the camp. All came to the lodge—men, women, and children—all came inside. "There is going to be medicine," he said. "Get some tallow," said he, "just a little." Then everyone looked for it. A long time they had to hunt before finding any. Then the woman rubbed the fat on the rock. It began to sing when she did it. It sang to the woman: "Take me, I am powerful." The people all saw it. The woman passed it to them, and they kissed it. "You shall have food," she said. Then she began to sing and then to dance. All joined in the dancing. They made a noise like buffalo. The woman sang, "A hundred I shall lead over the drive." She said, "When you sing, do not say more than a hundred." Now a man said when he sang, "Over a hundred shall I lead over the drive." The woman said, "We have made a mistake now. So many will go over that the enclosure will burst; they will jump out of it. There will be a solitary bull wandering through the camp tonight. It will be a mangy bull. No one shall kill him. If that bull comes tonight, we shall all be saved. If this rock falls on its face, then you will all be happy. There will be plenty of food." All went out. They were happy, because they were to receive food. The woman slept where the smudge was made. That rock made her powerful. He came through the camp, the one she said was coming—the mangy bull. They all knew him.

(CONTINUED)

They all said, "Ah-a-a! Don't kill him. Rub his back with firewood." In the morning all were happy because the mangy bull came at night. They did not kill him, the one that was said to come at night. When the woman looked out, that rock fell over on its face. Then she told them to be happy, because they would have something to eat. Looking up, the people saw many buffalo close to the camp. Then the swift young men went out and led the buffalo, many of them. They worked them into the lines. They frightened them to make them run swiftly. Then all ran over into the enclosure. Now the people ran there. Inside were the buffalo. So many were there that the enclosure was broken. Over a hundred were there. That is why they broke down the fence. Not many of them were killed. All the buffalo were bulls. That is why they broke down the fence.

The woman's husband took all the ribs and back-fat, saying, "With these shall a feast be made. Again my wife will make medicine." The people were somewhat happy, even though the number of animals killed was small. "For a little while we are saved. We have a little meat," said the man.

The next night it was called out again that the woman was to make medicine. This time she gave orders that only the women were to dance, so that cows might come to the drive. So the women danced. The men tried not to make another mistake. In the morning they looked from the hill again. They were made glad by the rock falling again on its face. Again the young men went out. Now all in the enclosure were cows. They were all killed with arrows. None of them got out. The people were happy now. They had plenty of meat. Everyone now believed in the power of the rock. The woman who found the rock was respected by her husband.

The Buffalo Rock, Northern Blackfeet

Wife of Little Plume
Blackfeet

Unknown beadworker
Apsaroke

IT WAS ABOUT a hundred years ago a man pitched his camp away from the other people. Now the man and his wife went out in different ways. They separated. As the woman was going along, she came to the place where Beavers were at work. The Beavers came out and invited her down to their lodge. When the man came home that night, he missed his wife and set out to find her. At last he discovered her tracks leading down into the water at the place where the Beavers were at work. Now he watched every day for her to appear. Every night when he was in the lodge he could hear dancing and singing. He could only hear it when inside of the lodge, but whenever he went outside he ceased to hear it. One evening when he came back from hunting, he found his wife at home in the lodge. She was burning incense. She had cleared a small spot back of the fire for this purpose. The man saw a large bundle at the back of the lodge, and as he looked at it the woman said, "That was given by the Beavers."

Now that night, when the man was sleeping, he dreamed about the Beavers. In his dream he saw the Beavers come into his lodge, and one of the Beavers addressed him, saying, "Now, my brother, you have the bundle and the medicine things; so you must learn the songs and how to paint." Then the Beavers taught him the songs, how to open the bundle, how to paint, etc. All the directions for the ceremony were given by the Beavers at this time. This was just as you will see it now, because we are about to open this bundle.

There was also another dream about this medicine. In this dream it was explained that the only women who can take part in the medicine lodge are those who have been true to their husbands. In this dream a headdress was given for the woman who makes a vow to give the Sun Dance. This was dreamed by the same man who received the medicine bundle from the Beaver. Afterwards he had another dream, in which the elk gave him a robe. This robe was to be used by the woman who gave the Sun Dance. Now, after this man had the dream about the elk, he took the robe and gave it to his wife, because she now had the headdress that is worn in the Sun Dance. She took the robe and wrapped it around the bundle in which the headdress was kept.

Tobacco is kept in the beaver medicine bundle, and this tobacco must be planted every year. The woman who plants the tobacco puts on the headdress and carries a digging stick. Songs are sung when the tobacco is planted. This is the way to raise the tobacco to be used in the beaver medicine.

Origin of the beaver medicine, Northern Piegan

IT WAS IN the very far north, at a place called The Place to Fall Off Without Difficulty. Some people were camped there. Among them was Chief Level Head, (other name, Buffalo Lodge Pole) who was trapping beaver. This man was a great hunter and trapper. He spent most of his time in this way. He had camped there before. His relatives wanted him to stay with them, but he would not; and, taking his wife, he went away and camped by himself. His wife was Otter Woman. One day he went out to hunt, and, on reaching camp with his meat on two dog travois, he called his wife to come out and get the meat. No one came. Then he, himself, took off the meat, untied the dogs, and went to look for her. As he went along he said, "I wonder if anything could have happened to her?" All this time he was tracking her along. At last he came to the place where she got water, and there he found her robe. There also was the pail made of paunch, her wooden cup, and bundle of wood. He saw tracks going down to the water. It was very deep. The man went into the water to follow the tracks, but lost them. He saw a beaver's house. He saw that these tracks led up to the beaver house. Then he knew for sure what had happened.

Then he went home and cried. He made up his mind that the beaver had run off with the woman; but he still cried and cried. He was there seven days, crying all the time. On the seventh day he thought to himself, "Tomorrow I will go home"; but that night he cried as before. But a man came to him, saying, "I have been sent to you. You are to fix up a lodge, for your wife is coming tomorrow. You must not look out when she comes." He heard the man sing, "Our walking is powerful, the man says," "My old home I am looking for it. It is powerful." (This means that the woman looked for her home.) Now while the woman was coming up, the strange man sang many such songs. These are the beaver songs. When the woman came out of the lake, she wore a medicine bonnet, and some head men [beavers] came out with her to help with the songs and to transfer the bundle. This party went into the lodge and transferred the bundle and the medicine bonnet to the woman and her husband. The tobacco plant and everything else was given with it. It took seven days to transfer the medicine.

Then the man and his wife went home, and the next summer he went out and planted his tobacco seeds as the beavers had directed. That year it grew well. Then he transferred the bundle to another man, and this man called in a friend to help him get it. Now it is over!

Otter Woman, Blackfeet

Susie Baggage
Oglala Lakota

Amitsei and Nakai Baldwin
Southern Cheyenne

MOST OF THE doctors are women, and they exercised great power in the art of curing most all diseases or cases of sickness.

Women doctors are made and educated, which comes about in a very peculiar way. Most of them begin quite young, and often the doctor will take one of her daughters that she selects along with her and begin by teaching her to smoke and help her in her attendance on the sick, and at the right time will commence with her at the sweathouse, while others will have a dream that they are doctors, and then the word will be given out. And in either case along in the late fall all will be made ready, the day being set.

The sweathouse (which is the white man's name and does not have the same meaning in our language; we call it <u>Ur-girk</u>) being selected, they take her to it, dressed with a heavy skirt that comes down to her ankles and which is made of the inner bark of the maple, with her arms and breast bare. They all go into the sweathouse. All begin to sing songs that are used for the occasion, dancing and jumping up and down, going slowly around the fire and to the right. They keep this up until she is wet with perspiration, as wet as the water could make her, and when she gets so tired that she can stand up no longer, one of her brothers or cousins takes her on his back with her arms around his neck and keeps her going until she is completely exhausted.

Sometimes she will be from three to ten years before being ready for the final graduation exercises, when she will be taken back to some almost inaccessible place on a high peak or on a very high rock where they will smoke, pray, and fast for from three to five days.

This girl is a virgin, as perfect in stature and active in movement and health as God can make her. She can bear hardships and punishment without complaint or murmur that would make a bear whine. When all is made ready to give her the final degree the time is set and word is sent all up and down the river, and at the appointed time many people will be there, some coming for many miles to see and take part in giving the young doctor her final degree. (CONTINUED)

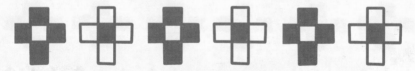

At sundown the fire is made in the center of the living room, and at the commencement of the hour of darkness she is brought in, goes through the door and down into the basement, takes her place, when the others that are to help her take their places, forming a circle around the fire, and all start singing in a low and monotonous voice, jumping up and down, the young doctor taking care of herself at first and taking instructions from the old doctor who sits close by but takes no part other than to instruct her. After keeping this up for two to four hours, the young doctor becomes very warm and fatigued, and they keep close watch of her until the time comes, when one of the men takes hold of her and holds her up and helps her to stand, still wearing her down, until two men take hold of her by each arm and in this way keep her dancing until she is helpless and so limp that she can no longer go on. Then they lay her up and out of the way, still keeping on with the ceremony until daylight in the morning, when all repair to their places to sleep for a few hours, then arise, go forth, bathe and eat and go back to their homes.

Che-na-wah Weitch-ah-wah (Lucy Thompson), Yurok

Good Woman and her
daughter Strikes Plenty
Oglala Lakota

Unknown
Absaroke

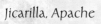

IN THE BEGINNING of the world there was an old man and an old woman. They had nothing to do and they prayed to the one who made the earth to give them something to live on. Then one day a spirit came and stood before them.

First he took them to a rock and said, "That is gold. It is worth much, but I cannot give it to you, for you do not know how to work it."

Then he showed them another rock, saying, "That is silver. That, too, is valuable, but you do not know of it or what to do with it, so I cannot give it to you. Some day people will come from across the ocean, from the east. They will feed you, give you clothes and food. That is why I will send them. And they will like this silver and gold."

Then the spirit took the old man and the old woman to the other side of the mountain. A big hole was there. "Go over there and dig out that clay," the spirit told the two old people. "I will show you how to make pots and bowls with it. You will live by this means."

Then the spirit called the woman over to him and touched both her hands with his, instructing her, "Now work the clay from your own knowledge and with your own understanding."

So the old man and woman went together to dig the clay and then the woman made a clay bowl and she did very good work. She made bowls of all shapes. But she did not know what to call the different bowls or the proper use for each shape.

That night the man and woman prayed and the spirit appeared to the woman in a dream and told her how to use the pots and what to call them. The spirit also told her that she must teach all the children what she knew.

Jicarilla, Apache

Unknown
Oglala Lakota

LONG AGO, THE Indians were traveling. And some old woman was among them. And it seems they did not like her.

Then it seems they spoke thus: "This old woman is good for nothing," they said. Then when they had spoken thus, "This old woman is good for nothing," they said, "therefore, let's abandon her," they said. Then they abandoned her.

Then it seems she wept. Then these Mountain Spirits came to her. And they spoke thus to her: "Why are you weeping?" they said to her.

"I weep because they have abandoned me," she said. "I cannot see, I cannot hear, and I cannot speak. For that reason, I weep."

Then they began to sing for her. And she who had been blind, her eyes were made to open. She who had been deaf began to hear again.

Then they spoke thus to her: "This that we have done is good. When you return, tell them about it," they said to her.

Then she performed all of the ceremony they had done for her in exactly their way. And in that way she returned.

Then she performed all of that which had been given to her in exactly their way. And, in this way, the ceremony came to be customarily performed.

Chiricahua Apache legend

THERE IS A very old woman who sits on the edge of a tall bluff. She is quilling a beautiful design on a buffalo robe. The woman is very old, so she tires easily. Beside her sits an ancient dog. He is so old that he has very few teeth. Even though he is old, he is still playful.

Every day the woman quills that buffalo robe. Soon she is tired and falls asleep. When she rests at night, the dog unravels all that she did the day before. If that dog forgets to unravel those quills, or gets too old, the old woman will finish the robe. That will be the end of the world.

Lucy Swan, Oglala Lakota

A MAN RODE by the house and said, "A tornado is coming, and it's coming right this way! You better leave, it's already killed animals and destroyed houses!" "No, I'll stay here!" Unci [Grandmother] said.

So then she went into the house and got her little pipe. When she was ready she came outside. By then the storm was close, the wind was blowing things around, and the dust made the air brown.

Grandma just pointed her pipe stem at that storm and prayed, "Grandfathers above and in the four directions, please hear me. Grandfathers above, spare this house, I'm praying! Grandfathers!" She prayed, and that storm split and went on either side, close by the house, but she was safe.

Lucy Swan, Oglala Lakota

Unknown
Oglala Lakota

I ADD MY breath to your breath
That our days may be long on the Earth
That the days of our people may be long
That we may be one person
That we may finish our roads together
May our Mother bless you with life
May our life paths be fulfilled.

Song from the Keres Indians of Laguna Pueblo

I WILL SOON leave you. I will return to the home whence I came. You will be to my people as myself; you will pass with them over the straight road; I will remain in my house below and will hear all that you say to me. I give you all my wisdom, my thoughts, my heart, and all. I fill your head with my mind.

Words of Corn Woman, <u>Iyatiku</u>, after she brought corn to the Keres Indians of Laguna Pueblo

IN THE BEGINNING Tse che nako, Thought Woman, finished everything, thoughts, and the names of all things. She finished also all the languages. And then our mothers, Uretsete and Naotsete said they would make names and they would make thoughts. Thus they said. Thus they did.

She (Tse che nako) is mother of us all; after Her, mother earth follows, in fertility, in holding, and taking us again back to her breast.

From the Keres Indians of Laguna Pueblo

THIS CORN IS my heart and it shall be to my people as milk from my breasts.

Prayer of Utset, the supernatural woman who brought corn to the Zia Pueblo

WAVING CORN WAS always in her cornfield, in which she built a strong scaffold to live and watch her corn. The Sun, falling in love with her, came down and sat by her side, saying, "I love you better than I love any other woman." She refused him, but the next day the Sun returned and sat beside her on the scaffold. Still she refused him, and sent him away three times.

"Very well, if you will not have me, you shall never taste of this fine field of corn!" the Sun said angrily.

"I will eat the corn; that is why I planted it," cried Waving Corn.

After that, the Sun shone so hot that the corn withered and sank to the ground. When darkness came, Waving Corn went over the field, wondering how to defeat the Sun. Suddenly, the corn rose up and was green as before. In the morning, a dense fog covered the earth, but at noon it walked away and the Sun shone hot on the land, and the cornstalks were dry and rattly. Again, as night came, Waving Corn walked forth and, as she touched it, the scared and wilted corn rose up. Four times this was done. At last, the Sun gave up and the corn prospered and was gathered and stored.

Mandan legend

Unknown
Oglala Lakota

Magpie family
Flatheads

REMEMBER THAT YOUR children are not your own, but are lent to you by the Creator.

Mohawk proverb

I CAN SAFELY say that the ultimate aim of Dakota life, stripped of accessories, was quite simple: One must obey kinship rules; one must be a good relative. No Dakota who has participated in that life will dispute that. In the last analysis every other consideration was secondary—property, personal ambition, glory, good times, life itself. Without that aim and the constant struggle to attain it, the people would no longer be Dakotas in truth. They would no longer even be human. To be a good Dakota, then, was to be humanized, civilized. And to be civilized was to keep the rules imposed by kinship for achieving civility, good manners, and a sense of responsibility toward every individual dealt with. Thus only was it possible to live communally with success; that is to say, with a minimum of friction and a maximum of good will.

The family unit of parents-and-child was not the final and complete idea it is elsewhere. It was an integral part of the larger family, the <u>tiyospaye</u> (clan), bound together with blood and marriage ties. The individuals constituting these larger groups bore definite relationships to each other and owed one another definite duties. They functioned as a unit, materially and spiritually, in a never-ending interplay of honorings one to another, young and old.

Ella Deloria, Yankton Dakota

WE AS INDIAN people have never forgotten the status of women. Those who have gotten away from the traditions may act as if they don't remember, but all of us know inside. Our memories are long, as long as the line of the generations. The elders have always passed on this knowledge. We have been told to never forget. So we remember and pass it on, too. With us there is no past, everything is now, and the only future is the generations to come.

So we continue the ceremonies. To participate in them is to participate in the circle of life, the whole circle—seen and unseen. They remind us to maintain balance, to live in peace with each other, to honor the Creator, the earth, and to acknowledge and show respect for the medicine powers.

Some people have no ceremony anymore. To have no ceremony is to fail to remember just where human beings are in the creation.

Anonymous Native American woman

...EVERYTHING ON THE earth has a purpose, every disease a herb to cure it, and every person a mission. This is the Indian theory of existence. Children were encouraged to develop strict discipline and a high regard for sharing. When a girl picked her first berries and dug her first roots, they were given away to an elder so she would share her future success. When a child carried water for the home, an elder would give compliments, pretending to taste meat in water carried by a boy or berries in that of a girl. The child was encouraged not to be lazy and to grow straight like a sapling.

Mourning Dove, Salish

HOW OFTEN HAVE we heard it reiterated that the destiny of the world depends on woman—that woman is the appointed agent of morality—the inspirer of those feelings and dispositions which form the moral nature of man. These remarks, although so common, are none the less true. The elevation of our race does depend upon the manner in which woman executes this commission. Nor does the destiny of man as an individual alone depend on female influence, but that of nations, kingdoms, and empires.

If this influence has been so universal in past ages, is it not equally powerful in our day. If so, how careful should the females of our little nation be in regard to the manner in which each one exerts her influence. The elevation of the Cherokee people also depends upon the females; and, perhaps, particularly upon those who are just springing into active life, and who enjoy the privileges of this institution. How necessary is it that each one of us should strive to rightly improve and discipline our minds while at school, and to be governed by principle and not by impulse, so that when we are called to other stations and our field of efforts widens, our influence may have an elevating and ennobling effect upon all with whom we come into contact.

Qua-Tsy, Cherokee

Ma-Kig-la
Oglala Lakota

MY FATHER HAD promised me to Goes Ahead, when I was thirteen. When I became sixteen years old my father kept his promise. I had not often spoken to Goes Ahead until he took me. Then I fell in love with him, because he loved me and was always kind. Young women did not then fall in love, and get married to please themselves, as they now do. They listened to their fathers, married the men selected for them, and this, I believe, is the best way. There were no deformed children born in those days and men and women were happier, too, I feel sure.

A man could not take a woman from his own clan, no matter how much he might wish to have her. He had to marry a woman belonging to another clan, and then all their children belonged to their mother's clan. This law kept our blood strong.

The happiest days of my life were spent following the buffalo herds over our beautiful country. My mother and father and Goes Ahead, my man, were all kind, and we were so happy. Then, when my children came I believed I had everything that was good on this world. There were always so many, many buffalo, plenty of good fat meat for everybody.

Pretty Shield, Absaroke

ᑢ ᑢ ᑢ ᑢ ᑢᑢ
ᑢ ᑢ ᑢ ᑢ ᑢ ᑢ

Lucy Pierre and daughter
Flathead

GIVING WAS GLORIFIED. The formal "give away" was a bona-fide Dakota institution. Naturally it followed that things changed hands with readiness when the occasion demanded, since the best teaching said things were less important than people; that pride lay in honoring relatives rather than in amassing goods for oneself; that a man who failed to participate in the giving customs was a suspicious character, something less than a human being.

If someone made you a gift, no matter how valuable it might be, he did not mean for it to grow old along with you. He expected you to use it when and as you chose to honor someone else, and, indirectly, yourself. He gave with that expectation, as much as to say, "I have owned this for some time. You own it next, and when you wish to make a gift, pass it on."

The teaching in the family, and in the <u>tiyospaye</u> (clan), was definitely in the direction of giving. One patriarch, when it came time to assemble gifts cooperatively to honor their dead, admonished his group thus: "My children, never skimp. Give adequately in a manner worthy of yourselves, or not at all. Give abundantly and with glorious abandon. Better not to honor someone than dishonor him by doing it haltingly and calculatingly. Pity the coward who gives half holding back, timid for his own private security because he does not put his faith in men but in mere chattel. My children, it is better to give and have nothing left, if need be, than to appear stingy. Property always flows back in due time to those who let it flow freely forth. In the endless process of giving, that is bound to be so." Such was the inherited belief by which the Dakota lived happy and satisfied all his days, and which he handed down to his children. They had grown up with it. Even the babies were imbued with it. "A man should be able to give without his pulse quickening," was a stock saying. The grateful recipients lauded the donor's name before the people as having done well. Before the Dakotas would appear small, they would let everything go, calmly, recklessly, should the occasion demand it. When, for instance, a warrior died in battle, his respect-relatives (sisters and women cousins) withheld nothing that might enhance his glory and memorialize his name. When a baby was born or a relative died, and honoring ceremonies were in order, once again gifts flowed freely. It was customary at a death to "throw away" property – everything belonging to the deceased and anything else the relatives had that they deemed worth giving.

Ella Deloria, Yankton Dakota

Wife of Louis Sitting Bull
Hunkpapa, Lakota

Wife of Yellowhair
Brule Lakota

MY MOTHER SPONSORED Sun Dances also. I grew up with that kind of life because she kept me close to her. That first time I vowed the Sun Dance I said I would fast for four days. That is the old way. At later Sun Dances they told me I would only have to fast for two days. Things have changed.

I was very young when I first started with this holy business, and now I am an old woman, on account of it. It has been a very trying life, especially during the medicine lodge ceremonies. Sometimes when I had to go out during the four days of rituals my assistants would have to hold me up, I would be so weak. I have always been devoted to my religious duties to help my family and people. All the younger people are like my children.

Yellow Buffalo Stone Woman, Blood

I HAVE HAD a beaver bundle for many years. It is the biggest medicine bundle of all the ones among our people. There is a very long ceremony for its opening, and they used to sing several hundred songs during it. The men and the women all join together to sing these songs and to dance with the different parts of the bundle. We imitate the bird and animal skins in them. We used to have a really happy time with this beaver ceremony, but now there is no one left who can lead it. I guess I have the last beaver bundle among the Bloods.

These things-that-sing [Blackfoot for radios and record players], I dislike them very much. When they are shut off I can still hear them going in my head. Sometimes when I'm in my room, praying, I feel like I'm trying to outdo those things. My daughter gets up and shuts it off and tells the kids around the house: "When your grandmother is praying you don't want to drown her words with your music." Then they listen, and I can hear myself.

Yellow Buffalo Stone Woman, Blood

THEY WEAR AN awl case to show they are industrious. They used this a long time ago to make clothes and tipis, everything. The little pouch is for a fire striker, to show they are hospitable and can make a warm home for family and visitors. They wear the knife case to symbolize generosity and the feeding of people. Today they might not have the awl inside [the little beaded case], but it means the same.

Lucy Swan, Lakota, explaining the traditional regalia worn by women

A CRIER WOULD ride through the village telling the people to be ready to move in the morning. In every lodge the children's eyes would begin to shine. Men would sit up to listen, women would go to their doors to hear where the next village would be set up, and then there would be glad talking until it was time to go to sleep. Long before the sun came the fires would be going in every lodge, the horses, hundreds of them, would come thundering in, and then everybody was very busy. Down would come the lodges, packs would be made, travois loaded. Ho! Away we would go, following the men, to some new camping ground, with our children playing around us. It was good hard work to get things packed up, and moving; and it was hard, fast work to get them in shape again, after we camped. But in between these times we rested on our traveling horses. Yes, and we women visited while we traveled. There was plenty of room on the plains then, so that many could ride abreast if they wished to. There was always danger of attack by our enemies, so that far ahead, on both sides, and behind us, there were our wolves (scouts) who guarded us against surprise as we traveled.

Ahh, my people were tough in those days. Tst, tst, tst! Now, when people get a little wet they build a fire and get dry again. In those old days when I was young, if in winter a person fell into icy water, he got out, took off his wet clothes, and rolled in the snow, rubbing his body with it, and got warm. Then, after squeezing out the water, he put on his clothes and forgot about getting wet. Yes, and the buffalo-runners rubbed their hands with snow and sand, so that their fingers would be nimble at handling the bow and arrows. Now my people wear gloves, and too many clothes. We are soft as mud.·

Pretty Shield, Absaroke

Pretty Shield
Absaroke

Unknown
Kootenai

FIRST, THE LITTLE baby through the medicine man's prayers has been
   given life,
Here and there, with the medicine man's song.
For the baby the songs have been sung.
Next, the baby's mother,
With the songs of the rain gods she has cared for the little baby.
Here and there the mother with the cloud cradle,
The little baby was cared for.
It was nice that the clouds came up like foam,
As if it was among those soft little clouds,
With this the baby was cared for.

Mother's song to a baby, Acoma

INDIAN PEOPLE LOVED their children above all else, for they were
the hope of the future and justification for the trials and tribulations of
their parents. They guaranteed the perpetuation of the family and continued the upholding of its honor. They were a special gift from the Creator
and the promise of a bright and happy future. They were the focus for
much of our time and attention, but they particularly spent time with their
grandparents, as these had both the most free time to devote to their care
and wisdom to pass on to the next generation. Their parents were in the
prime of life and were often too busy working and scouting up food to
give them the full attention they deserved. Our most important sense of
self and continuity, therefore, came from the very old, who were so kind,
gentle, considerate, and wise with us, particularly as children.

Mourning Dove, Salish

OUR SACRED TRANSFERS are the things that kept us the strongest in life. We believed in our religion, just like our old people handed it down to us. For every important thing they did in life there was a transfer—an initiation. Somebody that has already gone through that transfer and knows all about it, he will initiate a newcomer. It might be for a medicine pipe bundle, or it might be for a society bundle. These are things that we live by—the ceremonies and the meanings of these initiations teach us about life, so we try to learn them. It is just the same for a white man to study in school and learn about life. You make a living from it. Only they didn't work for money in the old days. They just worked for buffalo and enemy horses and nice belongings.

In our Indian life, [my husband] and I didn't just go ahead and do whatever we wanted. We took over these different medicine bundles, and each one has its own initiations. For instance, to make the holy moccasins worn for some ceremonies there is an initiation. There is another one for those moccasins to be mended. Then there is one for making the buckskin bags we keep sacred paint in. They make incense and they guide your hand to make all the first motions, for cutting, for sewing, and for finishing up. And all the while everyone is praying. Each time we get initiated like this, we get our face painted. That means you're given another thing to live by, and these things add up.

But today most of the people don't care much about these ways as they were given down to us. They want to do them just to suit themselves. Just to go with their own ideas about being Indians. They will make up holy things or say that they know about a ceremony, when they never had their faces painted for these things. They are making up their own ways and using the things handed down from the Creator. I am watching this going on around me and I think it is bad. And I am not shy to speak up and say what I think. I am an old woman, and I have been initiated and given the rights to many, many things in life. All the older Bloods know this. When I speak my mind some people may think that I am being bossy. But everyone knows that it is our tradition to back up what you say with your initiations. The leaders of the tribe always went through most of the transfer and took care of the main bundles. I have the rights to a lot of things that I don't even speak up about, because I don't want to make things too complicated. But we have to stick by the wisdom of our ancestors, and not try to outsmart them in talking about the Creator, and all that is created.

Paula Weasel Head, Blood

Wife of Bull Head
Oglala Lakota

THE WOMEN BY turns honored their men by taking cooked food, the best they had, to the council tipi. Directly it was taken from them, they hurried away. But don't assume that they were chased off. They left because it was considered unwomanly to push one's way into a gathering of the other sex; it was unmanly for men to do so under opposite circumstances. Outsiders seeing women keep to themselves have frequently expressed a snap judgment that they were regarded as inferior to the noble male. The simple fact is that woman had her own place and man his; they were not the same and neither inferior nor superior.

The sharing of work also was according to sex. Both had to work hard, for their life made severe demands. But neither expected the other to come and help outside the customary division of duties; each sex thought the other had enough to do. That did not mean, however, that a man disdained to do woman's work when necessary; or a woman, man's. The attitude on division of work was quite normal, however it looked to outsiders. A woman caring for children and doing all the work around the home thought herself no worse off than her husband who was compelled to risk his life continuously, hunting and remaining ever on guard against enemy attacks on his family.

Ella Deloria, Yankton Dakota

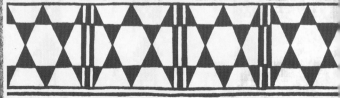

Daughter of Red Fish
Yanktonai Nakota

WE HIDATSA WOMEN had a kind of honor mark for industry, something like the honor marks the men had for striking the enemy.

If a girl was a worker and tanned hundreds of hides her aunt might give her an honor mark. My aunt Sage gave me such, a <u>maipsuka</u> or woman's belt. These were broad as a man's suspender and worked in beads, sometimes blue, sometimes with a cross design. One could not purchase or make such a belt; it had to be given.

For working a quill-decorated tent, a bracelet was given; for making a quill-embroidered robe, a ring. There were no other honor marks for industry, but these three.

Buffalo Bird Woman, Hidatsa

WHAT WE MIGHT call the formal education of Dakota youth was centered in the tribal ceremonies. The "sermons" recited on these occasions emphasized the ideals that each generation felt it vital to implant in the minds of its boys and girls.

Ella Deloria, Yankton Dakota

Daughter of Red Fish
Yanktonai Nakota

THOUGH I HEARD many strange experiences related by wayfarers, I loved best the evening meal, for that was the time old legends were told. I was always glad when the sun hung low in the west, for then my mother sent me to invite the neighboring old men and women to eat supper with us. Running all the way to the wigwams, I halted shyly at the entrances.

As each in turn began to tell a legend, I pillowed my head in my mother's lap; and lying flat upon my back, I watched the stars as they peeped down upon me, one by one. The increasing interest of the tale aroused me, and I sat up eagerly listening to every word. The old women made funny remarks, and laughed so heartily that I could not help joining them

Zitkala-Sa (Gertrude Bonnin)
Yankton Dakota

Bear Woman
Southern Cheyenne

THE GRANDFATHERS
and the grandmothers
are in the children:
teach them well.

Ojibwa proverb

MY FATHER WENT on talking to me in a low voice. That is how our people always talk to their children, so low and quiet, the child thinks he is dreaming. But he never forgets.

Maria Chona
Papago

A WEE CHILD toddling in a wonder world, I prefer to their dogma my excursions into the natural gardens where the voice of the Great Spirit is heard in the twittering of birds, the rippling of mighty waters, and the sweet breathing of flowers. Here, in a fleeting quiet, I am awakened by the fluttering robe of the Great Spirit. To my innermost consciousness the phenomenal universe is a royal mantle, vibrating with His divine Breath. Caught in its flowering fringes are the spangles and oscillating brilliance of sun, moon, and stars.

Zitkala-Sa (Gertrude Bonnin)
Yankton Dakota

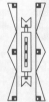

Unknown
Blackfeet

KIDS LEARNED A lot just through listening, watching, and then doing. Our folks didn't lecture us much. They'd tell stories, especially on the long winter nights. That's when we listened and learned what to fear, what to do, and what to respect. We learned that Old Man Coyote, <u>Esakuateh</u>, along with his little companion, Shedapay, shaped the world, making all the rivers, lakes, and mountains. He also put the stars in their places and made all the different birds and animals.

It was Old Man Coyote who gave us our Indian ways—how to live as Crows; how to dream, to hunt, to make tipis; and how to get medicine to live by. The old people told us about this. But Old Man Coyote was also a tricky person, and at times he could be real bad.

These winter stories taught us about the mysterious in life. Crows always believed that the mysterious was important in their lives. They fasted and cried so that a spirit person would adopt them and bring them good luck. But you had to follow their rules, or you came to harm.

Agnes Yellowtail Deernose
Absaroke

I AM NOT afraid; I have relatives.

Ella Deloria, Yankton Dakota

TRADITIONAL ADVICE TO women on getting married:

If you marry a man and you want to be certain of always retaining him, work for him. With work you will always be able to retain your hold on men. If you do your work to the satisfaction of your husband, he will never leave you. Remain faithful to your husband. Do not act as though you are married to a number of men at the same time. Lead a chaste life. If you do not listen to what I am telling you and you are unfaithful to your husband, all the men will jeer at you. They will say whatever they wish to [and no one will interfere].

Do not act haughtily to your husband. Whatever he tells you to do, do it. Kindness will be returned to you if you obey your husband, for he will treat you in the same manner.

If a wife has no real interest in her husband's welfare and possessions she will be to him no more than any other woman, and the world will ridicule her. If, on the other hand, you pay more attention to your husband than to your parents, your parents will leave you. Let your husband likewise take care of your parents, for they depend on him. Your parents were instrumental in getting you your husband, so remember that they expect some recompense for it, as likewise for the fact that they raised you.

When you visit your husband's people do not go around with a haughty air or act as if you considered yourself far above them. Try to get them to like you. If you are good-natured, you will be placed in charge of the home at which you happen to be visiting. Then your parents-in-law will tell your husband that their daughter-in-law is acting nicely to them.

Anonymous, Winnebago

Blackfeet women

Unknown
Tonto, Apache

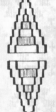

WHEN OUR GREAT Hozhooji Way is not being used anymore, Sa'a Naaghaii will take it away from us forever. Our people no longer observe even the smallest beliefs, such as daily rituals by which all the hogan tasks and habitual ways were done. I recall how the women got up before sunrise and took out the ashes, saying a prayer as they did so. When they finished cooking, the charcoal was poked back into the fire with a prayer of gratitude, and abundant blessings were asked that all the household members would walk the Blessing Way.

Stirring sticks used to stir mush were objects of prayers; each time they were used the user offered up a prayer. Even children were taught rituals. When a child lost a milk tooth he ran outside with it, closed his eyes, turned his face away and threw the tooth over his right shoulder toward the east with these words, "May I eat a fat gopher with the new one." This was done so he would grow a strong tooth that would last to old age.

In early times Dine'e were very religious; they were zealous with all their rituals. They went out before sunrise with their pollen to pray, especially after a bad dream.

Dine'e religion is for healing the sick of body and mind. Intricate chants to drive out evil spirits and resist witches and ghosts, numerous sand paintings, prayers, and blessings to please the gods – all these are part of the ritual for the many different ceremonies that make up the Hozhooji Way.

The People believe in one great divine Supreme Being and in a good universe, so Dine'e want to live a good life. They also believe there are forms of witchcraft and sorcery. These were very much in use during primitive days but are now almost stamped out, though one still hears rumors about witchcraft.

Dine'e religion is big, filled with reverence for the Great Spirit who has control over all. Dine'e found everlasting peace in some things they did; their findings confirmed their customs. So we should say little or nothing against their religion. Many present-day medicine men practice the ceremonies to heal those sick in body and mind. To me it is like having first the light of fire, then the candle, oil, gas, and finally electricity to shed an even broader light.

Irene Stewart, Navajo (Dine'e)

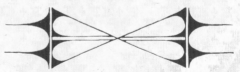

WOMEN HAVE POWER. Men have to dream to get power from the spirits and they think of everything they can hoping that the spirits will notice them and give them some power. But we have power. Children. Can any warrior make a child, no matter how brave and wonderful he is?

Maria Chona, Papago

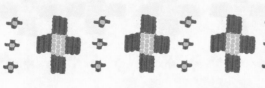

IT WAS THE CUSTOM when you loved a child to have the baby's ears pierced, especially the first born child. A horse was given to have this done. This is how my son first gave away. He was about one year old at the time. He cost us the loss of many things, horses, etc. He was on many committees when he was young, and his father gave away many horses at give-aways, sometimes three or four or five. His father did this because he loved him. This is when I learned to love the give-away and I still like to give.

Once they had a dance in Lame Deer with many small boys and girls dancing on the outside circle. When the singers stopped, old man Strange Owl announced: "Come and pick out your children and give away for them because they like to dance." He was a great man.

Belle Highwalking, Northern Cheyenne

A NATION IS not conquered until the hearts of its women are on the ground. Then, no matter how brave its warriors nor how strong their weapons, it is done.

Cheyenne proverb

THE HEART OF the family is the mother because life comes from her.

Onondaga Proverb

*Unknown family
Southern Cheyenne*

WHEN I WAS the Pipe child, whenever my mother took the Pipe bundle outside of the lodge, I took the tripod out after her. I was told how to set the tripod when the camp was about to move, with two of the legs close together and the third far out. Whenever my father made smudge with pine needles, he would give me some and I would chew them and would hold my hands over the smudge. Then I would rub my left palm up my right arm, my right palm up my left arm, then both palms from the top of my head down the sides of my neck and down my breast.

I did not have any duties beyond helping my mother when she brought the Pipe bundle out and brought it in.

If anybody vowed to be painted by the keeper, I would be present at the rite next to my mother and sit there through the ceremony.

Whenever while I was the Pipe child I got sick my father would put pine needles on me, and then he would take down the bundle and put it on my parents' bed, and would say to me: "Put your arms around your brother [the Pipe] and pray to your brother so you may get well." The Pipe keeper and his wife claim the Feathered Pipe as their son and tell their children that the Pipe is their brother. When I put my arms around the Pipe I was told to say to the Pipe: "My dear brother, have pity on me, that I may get well of my illness." Of course the Pipe was not human but because I was a baby when my father got it, I grew up with it and thought just as much of it as of my own blood relatives.

When while I was Pipe child I had been out playing and in the evening would come home and see the Pipe bundle over the door, I would stand and look at it a long time and would say: "Feathered Pipe, I am going into our lodge now."

My father used to tell me: "This Pipe was given by the Supreme Being through Bha'a. The Supreme Being is the father of the Pipe."

Garter Snake, Gros Ventre

Beads
Oglala Lakota

Wife of American Horse
Oglala, Lakota

WHEN YOU GROW up and finally have your own home, pity the old men and pity the old women, pity the poor. If you see an old woman with a ragged dress, give her a blanket. Make moccasins for these old women. If you do that the One Above who watches and looks at you doing those things is going to reward you.

Gros Ventre

THE PRAYERS TO the sun were the most ardent of all. In the annual Sun Dance, which lasted many days, everything was done in decency and order. Time was taken for it. There was no hurry because this was the whole of life. Nothing was so important as that those men who had cried out to God in their distress during the year should offer themselves here, votive offerings in fulfillment of their pledge. This was the great corporate prayer, the highlight of Dakota life. So the people followed in droves to wherever the next of many successive preliminary rites was to take place. They attended the ceremonial setting up of the Sun Dance booth. They watched the "man of gentle speech" as he dug the hole where the sacred pole, as a symbol of life, would stand in the center of the dance, and then as he buried at its base certain requisite gifts. He had been chosen out of honor. Every task assigned was an honor and given to the worthy. There was no buying one's way in.

The Sun Dance itself was terribly moving. Men carried out in exact detail the vows that they had made to the <u>Wakan</u> (sacred): that they would give one hundred pieces of their living flesh, or would pierce their chest or back muscles with skewers and attach themselves by ropes to the sacred pole and dance so. It was a bloody and tearful sight. Not that the victims wept, but their respectful relatives—their sisters and cousins—and their mothers and aunts and grandmothers did so. It must be understood that all suffering was self-dictated and self-imposed. No man ever told another how he should scarify and torture himself in order to pray; nor yet that he should desist, once he had made a promise to God.

The climax came just before dawn, the last dawn after a vigil of forty-eight hours or more, when finally the dancers could properly stop and were led staggering away to rest on their sagebrush couches. Then the holy man, the leader, came to the pole and clasped it tightly with both arms, letting the rest of his body hang inert as with emotions unutterable he wailed ceremonially on behalf of all the people. His role was to wail an entreaty to the <u>Wakan</u> through the sun. He wailed importunately, like a child insisting on a favor; he wailed that all the hopes and desires and all the private prayers of all hearts might be realized.

It was an unspeakably holy moment, the holiest in the life of these people. It touched them deeply, for it had to do with their very existence. Some who had desperate needs—a dying child to be restored, and so on—wept softly. When the wailing man had finished he seated himself by the buffalo-skull altar at the base of the pole, fixed his eyes on

(continued)

the eastern sky, and waited. And the people also turned to watch, all in awesome silence. Then, presently, after a colorful promise, there was the sun once again! Dazzling, powerful, unfailing—no wonder the Dakotas thought it holy! It was. And it was so personal, too. Quickly it sought them all out, great or small, and warmed each one most pleasantly and individually at the one instant, impartially. Everyone sighed with satisfaction. Avoiding common talk, they dispersed in all directions toward their tipis for another year, confident that ill would skirt their borders because they had done their part beautifully and well.

Ella Deloria, Yankton Dakota

THE GREATEST OF all deities among the tribes of North America was the sweat lodge. Its use was universal among the people of the forest, and many tribes still hold fast to its traditional sacredness. The Colville tribes were no exception, since they cherished a belief in this spirit of ancestral legends.

During times of affliction or troubles in life, the Indian always turned to the sweat lodge to make a prayerful appeal. It was a place that made no distinctions. All could go there: rich or poor, weak or strong, simple-minded or great in knowledge, commoner or chief, uneducated or adept in shamanistic wisdom. All were equal to enter the lodge to pray and worship our Creator. There were no lines drawn between any of them: male or female, old or young. All had the same privileges to enter a church open to the public, regardless of race.

Mourning Dove, Salish

Juanity Bahad
Navaho

FIRST OF ALL *we must know something of the terms they used. The basic Dakota word in this area is* <u>Wakan</u>*. God is* <u>Wakan</u>*. By whatever name a people may call him, he is still the same. I mean that Almighty Power, invisible, but nonetheless real, even to the most primitive. They feel there is a Power greater than themselves, which in all ages and all climes they strive somehow to understand. The Dakotas called him by various terms:* <u>Wakan</u> *(Holy, Mysterious, Magical, Inscrutable);* <u>Taku-Wakan</u> *(Something-Holy);* <u>Taku-Skanskan</u> *(Something-in-Movement);* <u>Wakan</u> <u>Tanka</u> *(Great Holy—commonly translated as the Great Spirit); and, finally,* <u>Wahupa</u>*, an untranslatable term in the sacred language of the esoteric.*

Of course, it cannot be said of any race that every single member of it is occupied with religious speculation and aspiration to the exclusion of all other subjects. Nevertheless, it was a Dakota trait to be religious, always subconsciously aware of the Supernatural Power. Before it, they felt helpless and humble. It was not smart to try to conquer that Power, or to defy or blaspheme it. They did not speak flippantly of it while they were safe and gay, and then have to turn about and run right back to it when they were frightened. That was unsportsmanlike; it was undignified, too. And if your Dakota wanted to be any one thing, it was to be dignified at all times. The people were imbued with some age-old wisdom that said all men must bow to the <u>Wakan</u>*, anyway, so it is best to stay bowed and not have to bow perforce.*

Though I talked with them at different times, and individually for the most part, my informants all felt that it was an error to say the Dakotas actually worshipped rocks, trees, the four winds, and other manifestations of nature. "They are not themselves <u>Wakan</u>*, but the* <u>Wakan</u> *is in all things."*

Most prayers were made to a rational medium of <u>Wakan</u> *that could be counted on to answer with due respect, honor, and dignity as a man to his relative. The river was always implored as the giver of beauty. The four winds and the earth and the sun were all benevolent mediums.*

Ella Deloria, Yankton Dakota

Black Tongue
Lakota

FOR CENTURIES, RELIGION had determined the entire structure of Hopi life. To them, life was a constant prayer to the Creator, the Great Spirit. Not just one day a week, but every day, was a day of prayer to the Hopi. They could not be changed overnight.

Polingaysi had watched the old men meditating on the rooftops, wrapped in their blankets. She had seen them cast the blankets aside as the sun rose, had seen them rise and reach out to the sun's rays and press that outpouring of energy to their bodies. Her mother had told her they were praying for health and wisdom, so she too prayed for health and wisdom, bringing the sun's rays to her with passion and bathing herself in them with slow strokings of her brown hands and complete faith in their efficacy. Against the invading white man the Hopis had no other defense. Prayer, prayer alone, was their refuge.

Placing her thin hand on Polingaysi's head her mother looked into the girl's sympathetic eyes. "I tell you, Polingaysi, you will live to see a time when the <u>dotsi</u>, our soft buckskin moccasin, is no longer worn. My own grandmother once told me there would some day be a path made in the heavens and along it people would travel as do the eagles. She said, too, that people would move swiftly, their feet not touching the ground. And she had never seen a man on horseback.

"She said that in that time the Hopis would no longer walk quietly, single file, along their ancient streets, but that they would walk side by side, uttering bad words in loud voices, as the boys and girls are doing today. Girls would conceive before their time of womanhood was proved, and unknown diseases would mystify the Man With Eyes, whose duty it is to heal.

"Minds would be confused. Strangers would dig in our fallen-in ancestral homes and shake the garments of the ancients. We have seen this prediction come to pass.

"When these things happen," Grandmother had said, "it will be the time of _Suh-ah-kits-pe-oo-tani_, the time when changes come swiftly, and that will be the forerunner of the end of an age."

Polingaysi Qoyawayma (Elizabeth White), Hopi

WE DO NOT walk alone. Great Being walks beside us. Know this and be grateful.

Polingaysi Qoyawayma (Elizabeth White), Hopi

Unknown
Shoshone (left)

Wife of Left Hand
and child
Oglala Lakota (right)

THE WHITES HAVE not waited to find out how good the Indians were, and what ideas they had of God, just like those of Jesus, who called him Father, just as my people do, and told men to do to others as they would be done by, just as my people teach their children to do. My people teach their children never to make fun of any one, no matter how they look. If you see your brother or sister doing something wrong, look away, or go away from them. If you make fun of bad persons, you make yourself beneath them. Be kind to all, both poor and rich, and feed all that come to your wigwam, and your name can be spoken of by every one far and near. In this way you will make many friends for yourself. Be kind both to bad and good, for you don't know your own heart. This is the way my people teach their children. It was handed down from father to son for many generations. I never in my life saw our children rude as I have seen white children and grown people in the streets.

The chief's tent is the largest tent, and it is the council tent, where every one goes who wants advice. In the evenings the head men go there to discuss everything, for the chiefs do not rule like tyrants; they discuss everything with their people, as a father would in his family. Often they sit up all night. They discuss the doings of all, if they need to be advised. If a boy is not doing well they talk that over, and if the women are interested they can share in the talks. If there is not room enough inside, they all go out of doors, and make it a great circle. The men are in the inner circle, for there would be too much smoke for the women inside. The men never talk without smoking first. The women sit behind them in another circle, and if the children wish to hear, they can be there too. The women know as much as the men do, and their advice is often asked. We have a republic as well as you. The council tent is our Congress, and anybody can speak who has anything to say, women and all. They are always interested in what their husbands are doing and thinking about. And they take some part even in the wars. They are always near at hand when fighting is going on, ready to snatch their husbands up and carry them off if wounded or killed. One splendid woman that my brother Lee married after his first wife died, went out into the battlefield after her uncle was killed, and went into the front ranks and cheered the men on.

(CONTINUED)

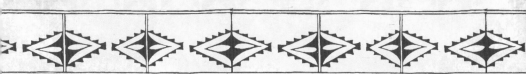

Her uncle's horse was dressed in a splendid robe made of eagles' feathers and she snatched it off and swung it in the face of the enemy, who always carry off everything they find, as much as to say, "You can't have that — I have it safe"; and she stayed and took her uncle's place, as brave as any of the men.

It means something when the women promise their fathers to make their husbands themselves. They faithfully keep with them in all the dangers they can share. They not only take care of their children together, but they do everything together; and when they grow blind they take sweet care of one another. Marriage is a sweet thing when people love each other. If women could go into your Congress I think justice would soon be done to the Indians. I can't tell about all Indians; but I know my own people are kind to everybody that does not do them harm; but they will not be imposed upon, and when people are too bad they rise up and resist them. This seems to me all right. It is different from being revengeful. There is nothing cruel about our people. They never scalped a human being.

Sarah Winnemucca, Piute

I AM AN OLD woman now. The buffaloes and black-tail deer are gone, and our Indian ways are almost gone. Sometimes I find it hard to believe that I ever lived them. My little son grew up in the white man's school. He can read books, and he owns cattle and has a farm. He is a leader among our Hidatsa people, helping teach them to follow the white man's road. He is kind to me. We no longer live in an earth lodge, but in a house with chimneys, and my son's wife cooks by a stove. But for me, I cannot forget our old ways. Often in summer I rise at daybreak and steal out to the corn fields, and as I hoe the corn I sing to it, as we did when I was young. No one cares for our corn songs now. Sometimes in the evening I sit, looking out on the big Missouri. The sun sets, and dusk steals over the water. In the shadows I seem again to see our Indian village, with smoke curling upward from the earth lodges, and in the river's roar I hear the yells of the warriors, and the laughter of little children as of old. It is but an old woman's dream. Then I see but shadows and hear only the roar of the river, and tears come into my eyes. Our Indian life, I know, is gone forever.

Waheenee, Hidatsa

Julia Wades in the Water
Blackfeet

Little Hawk Woman
Absaroke

BY JUNE PEOPLE are looking forward to the Sun Dance. The Sun Dance draws a lot of people from all districts.

Building the dance lodge takes all day, and the dancers go in after the sun goes down and a full moon is coming up in the east. A lodge pole that runs from the west edge directly east is known as the Chief's Pole. It is forked with two green tips, and they put an eagle there as in a nest. The eagle is Grandfather Sun's messenger, and the pledger and medicine man share this pole in sending prayers and receiving messages from the Sun. The main power comes from the Creator, the one the Crow call <u>Acbadadea</u>, The Maker of Everything.

The dancers suffer without food or water for two and a half days, running at the buffalo head attached to the center tree and dancing back to their places. While dancing, they blow their prayers through an eagle-bone whistle to the Creator, or to Grandfather Sun, according to their belief. They also offer tobacco in a smoke prayer at the tree. If the buffalo on the center tree knocks a dancer down, he expects to get a gift of power, perhaps a power to cure.

The second day is the hardest, and relatives bring sweet-smelling sage and cattails for the dancers' beds. Everyone tries to help the dancers who are sacrificing themselves in this way of prayer, so they can change their luck or to help a loved one get through a sickness. On this second day the dancers feel the dryness of their throats, and the suffering without food and water under the hot sun makes them very tired. But they dance hard and pray with sincerity so they will be blessed. Most people like to be doctored on the second day, for the medicine man can draw strong power from the tree for their cures.

Every morning at sunrise the dancers line up to greet Grandfather Sun. The power is close now, and the dancers pray to be free from their aches and pains, and they pray for those who are dear to them. The pledger gives a special prayer as the Sun casts his powers over the sacred fire. An elder first clears the way of all evil with a cedar prayer, and then the pledger can offer his tobacco prayer. He prays for the dancers and their wishes, for the sick, and that the old people may live longer. He asks that children grow up healthy and that his own wishes be granted. He also prays for the government and people of the United States.

The Sun Dance ends on the morning of the third day when the dancers take water brought by a virtuous woman and blessed by respected old men. No dancer leaves until he has asked a clan uncle or aunt to pray

(CONTINUED)

for him. They used the Sun Dance a lot during the war to bring our Crow boys safely home, and we lost only two of our boys. During the war a few old men and women fasted, and some men pledged to dance or to fast in every Sun Dance until the war was over. That might mean sacrificing themselves in three or four Sun Dances a year.

The Sun Dance changed during the fifties, and women made the biggest change when they danced and prayed with eagle-bone whistles just like the men. Today there are almost as many women dancers as men. In the lodge, men and women dancers are kept separate. Men and women are separated in the lodge because in Crow belief "medicine fathers" with sacred power to give do not like to be around women who are having a menstrual flow. To make sure that there is no interference with the sacred power, any woman having her period is required to leave the dance lodge, whether a dancer or an onlooker.

Agnes Yellowtail Deernose, Absaroke

TO PROTECT THEIR newborn, the Crow people also used a name blessing that could bring good health and prosperity to the child. They invited a man known to have powers (usually an outstanding warrior, and often a clansman of the father), to give a name blessing at the time when the ears were pierced. This usually was done for a boy child. After the naming the father would invite his clan brothers to a feast, and these men would tell of their dreams. Their summer dreams always looked ahead to winter when snow was on the ground, and their winter dreams always looked ahead to the time when the grass was green and it was warm. That is how they protected their children from year to year with dream blessings. An Indian name given by a clan uncle or a well-known clan brother is still considered important to the health and the success of Crow children.

Agnes Yellowtail Deernose, Absaroke

THE DOWNY FEATHERS of an eagle, or of any other bird, are called "breath feathers." Striking an armed enemy with a bow, coup-stick, lance, or with the hand, or disarming him, without injury, counted as the most honorable of coups. Killing and scalping an enemy did not entitle a warrior to count a coup.

Pretty Shield, Absaroke

Unknown
Absaroke

Rosy White Thunder
Brule Lakota

THE WOMEN EMERGING are
the hearts of the nations.

Megisi, Turtle Mountain Ojibway

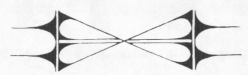

A GIRL ALWAYS started her fast at the first sign of menstruation, usually at an age between twelve and fifteen. She was regarded as immediately contaminated and not allowed to come in contact with her family for ten days. When she did return, she had to take several sweat baths and put on a complete change of clothing. The discarded clothing was tied in a bundle and put in the fork of a tree near the menstrual tipi.

In the old days, no village was complete without such shelters reserved especially for the women during their periods. They were usually located downstream so as not to pollute the water used for cooking and drinking. Men absolutely shunned the women at this time. They were believed to cause ill luck and sickness to any man who came in contact with them.

Fasting youths had to bathe each morning at the first streak of dawn. While in this solitary retirement, they dried off with spiny fir boughs to become strong and healthy.

A girl prayed about motherhood at this time. Although she had to stay away from the sweat lodge and from hunting, fishing, and gambling gear, she could pick berries and dig up roots. She could not pick herbs or make love potions. She stayed away from camp, but if she had to go there, she never went behind a tipi or stepped near the head of a bed. If she came near someone already ill, she might make that person die.

The girl was purified when she returned and stayed in her parents' tipi, thereafter rigidly chaperoned. She was wrapped in a virgin's cape so men could not see her body.

After a girl returned from the isolation of the menstrual hut, [the culmination of] her intensive spiritual training, she was looked upon as a woman of value.

Mourning Dove, Salish

LOLOLOMA, THE BEAR Clan chieftain, is responsible for the well-being of our village, and must make a daily pathway for us, his people, through prayer. He calls us his children. We call him our father. He prays for long life, purity, abundant crops, for all of us who live in Oraibi. He prays for rain. He prays for the essence of good in the plants we use, and in the clay we dig and crush for our pottery making, and in the rocks we pile one on top of the other in house building.

Your father and I are responsible for the well-being of our own home and our children. It is our duty to see to it that our children have a place to live and food to nourish their bodies. It is Lololoma's duty to see to it that we are all fed spiritually. That is why he prays in the mornings, and again in the evenings. He is the father of our spiritual home.

Sevenka (mother of Polingaysi), Hopi

THE AIM OF the old Dakota economic system and that of the white man's are one and the same, incongruous as that sounds when we compare the two systems for achieving it. Security, that was the aim: food, clothing, shelter, and an old age free from want. All peoples need that; it is what they struggle for in their respective ways.

But the two systems in question are irreconcilable. They go counter to each other. One says in effect: "Get, get, get now; all you can, as you can, for yourself, and so insure security for yourself. If all will do this, then everyone will be safe." And it depends on things, primarily.

The other said: "Give, give, give to others. Let gifts flow freely out and they will flow freely back to you again. In the universal and endless stream of giving this is bound to be so." And that system depended on human beings—friends, relatives.

Ella Deloria, Yankton Dakota

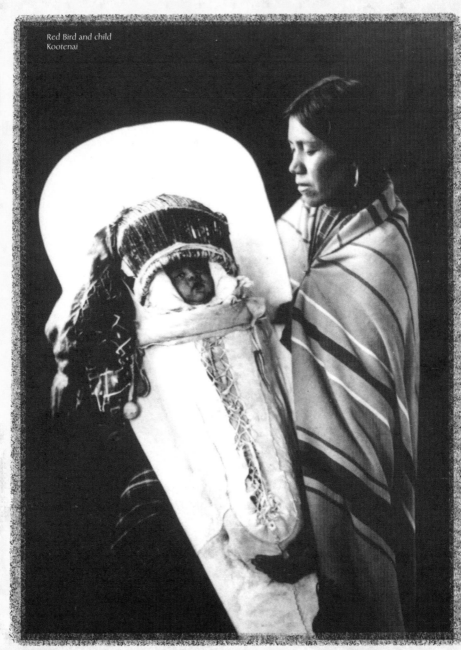

Red Bird and child
Kootenai

Unknown
Apsaroke

THE TRADITIONAL IMPORTANCE of the native doctor among our people gave parents an enticement for sending their children out into the forest each night to hunt for a supernatural spirit and become accomplished shamans. An Indian doctor, with the knowledge of spirit guardians and animal guides, had greater influence among the natives than did the chief, [especially] if he was a good medicine man with one or more powerful spirits.

A child might find these supernatural powers almost any place: water, cliffs, forest, mountains, remains of lightning-struck trees, animal carcasses, old campfires, or the sweat lodge itself. The spirits were supposed to appear to a child when they were impressed by the dedication and lured by the purity of the persistent seeker.

[The spirit's] appearance came to a child in a vision, in the form of an animal or an object that spoke about how the spirit would help him or her in future life, especially when needed during times of distress. It sang its spiritual song for the child to memorize and use when calling upon the spirit guardian as an adult. Such a vision did not always come to a child while awake. Sometimes it came while the child was asleep beside the token he or she had been given.

Indian theory holds that each spirit has the same strengths as its animal counterpart, as judged by close observation of nature and the outcome of actual fights, in "real" life, between such animals or shamans with their powers.

Ever since I was seven years old, my parents, my adopted grandmother, Teequalt, and other relatives had coached me to hunt for the spiritual blessings of a medicine woman. I followed the rules and never was afraid to go after water or run other errands at night, the time to search for a vision to accomplish my goal. I used to get up at dawn and bathe in cold water. At first I resented this, but I grew to like it afterward. I remember that my feet would stick to the ice, when I got out of the hole chopped into the stream where we took our morning baths during winter. People used to bathtubs and plenty of hot water might think this terrible, but it is a refreshing sensation. Getting out, the water feels warm against the frigid air, creating a sensation that penetrates the body and makes a person feel like running and jumping. It is a great preventive against the common cold; usually a person taking this daily bath is always healthy and long-lived.

Mourning Dove, Salish

Unknown
Kiowa

THE OLD TIMES were good times, when everyone lived on their own places. In those days people lived all over the reservation and in the hills, and they traveled back and forth on horseback and on wagons. The old people made their homes wherever they had land and I never forgot how life was then. I think about all these things now that I am old.

It was different in the past before people owned cars. Each family lived at their place and farmed their own land. It was when the cars came that people became wild and now no one recognizes their relatives. They just drive past their relative's place. When we used to travel by wagons, we would stop along the way with our relatives and visit for several days or overnight. We visited a lot and loved one another very much. But this is all gone now and no one knows how they are related to one another.

Life is so different at this time. We live bunched in towns and it is here that people make their homes. No one wants to live in the country anymore. There are even some old people today that always lived in town, and their children in turn grew up in town, and they will never have known what it was like to live in the country.

It must have been really good in the old times. When I was young, I used to hear the old people talk about those times. They said it was good when they camped and roamed on the plains, so it must be true.

I think about the way I used to live, when we gathered berries and wild food and ate rabbits, grouse, porcupine, and beaver. It was a good life, eating what you gathered and eating dried meat. Later people began to plant gardens, especially potatoes and corn. We made dried corn and also the old ladies hung up dried pumpkins which we cooked with corn. We ate everything and it made us strong. We had strong teeth and no one was toothless. Since we eat white man's food now, we have become toothless and wear dentures. No one got discouraged or was lazy and we did not see hard times. No one drank or fought one another in those days.

Belle Highwalking, Northern Cheyenne

THE INDIANS WHO had always lived the life of integrity on earth, when they die, their souls or spirit travels a narrow and winding trail which takes the soul north, to a land far away from their native haunts. This far northern clime is said to be the old land of Cheek-cheek-alth, where the spirit finds a ladder that reaches from earth into Heaven. As the spirit climbs the ladder to Heaven, it reaches God on that infinite shore, where it dwells forever in flowery fields of light, staying together with the Master in peace and love, and joining the spirits of those that have gone before them.

Can you of the Christian faith comprehend why we take so kindly to your own belief? Yet we think that ours is the most perfect; and yet you call us savage. We love our God almost akin to sadness and are always ready with a prayer offering, be it midday hour or in the hours of the silent night. The Indian in all his savagery could never blaspheme the sacred name of his Creator in man's built houses or in his daily life, as he is a child of nature, akin to nature's God, [believing] that the Divine Being is the beacon light of his soul, showing him life beyond the grave and [leading him] into the flowery fields of light and love, on that infinite shore, into the glories of Heaven.

Woman was manifestly the upholder of her race, loved as the unassuming creature who gave to the race clean-limbed and vigorous men. But ah, the sad knell, the approach of civilized man, and his crushing hand of debauchery, to the sorrow of our race; and our laws have long since been demolished, and with it our true religion, our life-blood, our all. Out of the gloom of saddened years, rising in scattered remnants, like the children of Israel that have lived without a country for many weary centuries, we are struggling to gain our own once more: freedom to worship God in our own way and to be allowed to become citizens of this, our own glorious country.

Che-na-wah Weitch-ah-wah (Lucy Thompson), Yurok

*Unknown
Blackfeet*

I WAS READY to spend ten days in the mountain wilderness as a young woman. This was my last preparation for a future as a renowned medicine woman.

When I got to the base of the mountain, I picked up two stones and put them inside my dress above the belt. I went quickly up the slope without stopping until I was almost at the top. As I had been taught, I loosened my belt and let the first stone drop, saying, "When I have children, that is the way they will come, with me on the run." I dropped the second stone at the top and said, "This is the way the afterbirth of the child will come. I will never have trouble bearing my children."

I continued to follow the teachings. When I washed my face in the creek, I would use fir boughs to dry off so my hands did not touch my face. Otherwise I would wrinkle early in life. I blew a breath toward the rising sun and whispered, "May the Great Spirit protect my youth for many years to come." I rubbed my hands and feet with the green boughs, blowing first to the sun and then to my fingertips and toes, praying they would remain small and unwrinkled.

I never touched my hair with my hands, only with the comb. I would groom myself each dawn beside mountain streams and greet the rising sun either by sitting and looking toward it or by standing with arms extended in deep prayer. I prayed for future success, always ending with, "May the Great Spirit and Creator spare my life from accidents, illness, deformity, and laziness. Bless me with a long and prosperous life. Make me, dear God of the Heavens, to be honest and strong in character, to face life with an honorable, truthful, and strong will, without fearing man or beast."

Mourning Dove, Salish

IN THE EVENING we kids could not run around and make much noise in the house because every night father would smoke a peace pipe and pray. When father had a visitor, mother used to keep us quiet by telling us stories, and sometimes she would tell us a story or legend. At other times we would lie down on the floor with our friends and take turns telling stories instead of chasing each other around. We told stories about horses, beavers, coyotes, and birds. Grandma Stays By the Water told us many of these stories, and she also sang lullabies that told us about the different animals and their habits.

Old men used to get together regularly in the evening to smoke and pray. The men always sat toward the back and the women and kids up by the door. This was the way it was in the old days in the tipi. The place of honor, and the place where a man hung his medicine, was in the back of the tipi. Here he received his guests, and whatever they had to do together, they first opened with a smoke prayer. When father and [his friends] smoked, they pointed the pipe to the Star People and to Mother Earth and the Earth People. Then they pointed to where the winds came from, first the north, then the south, and said the same thing. I think this tobacco smoking to the stars and cold and warm winds was meant to take care of everything, to keep us strong and healthy and to protect us from harm during the winter.

Kids were around the old people a lot, and we learned to respect them and what they were doing and saying. When they were smoking and praying, they were pretty strict, and we were not allowed to walk in front of them but had to pass around at the back. We noticed how the old men would make a circuit to the left of the stove when they were leaving, the same as they used to do when leaving the tipi. I think kids today would be smart if they listened more to older people and learned from them. Now, young people are busy running around in cars, and they don't want to listen or pay attention to older people.

Agnes Yellowtail Deernose, Absaroke

Unknown
Inuit

Unknown
Lakota

WITH THE INDIAN way, you don't have to go to church in order to pray. You can step outside, anytime. When I'm smoking, sometimes I'm praying with my cigarette. As much as I smoke, half the time there's a little prayer that goes out for somebody or something....

I can sit under my pine trees here and offer my prayers, and my prayers are answered. I don't have to go into a church or cathedral just on Sunday. I can go out two or three times a day. If something bothers me, I can go out there and pray and I'm sure I'm being heard. It's a portable church. As far as I'm concerned, there is no better church here on this place except under these pine trees.

Susie (Walking Bear) Yellowtail, Absaroke

IF YOU LOOKED into such a tipi of the past as I am talking about, you might see only the surface untidiness—the unavoidable dirt, discomfort, and inconvenience incident to primitive life lived on the ground. Those would be the obvious features, and you might come away thinking that was all. And that would be a pity, for underneath that surface lay something very wonderful—the spiritual life of a patient, unselfish, and courteous people who disciplined themselves without letup to keep the tribal ideal at all costs.

Ella Deloria, Yankton Dakota

CALMLY, MY MOTHER explained: "A small portion of food is being prepared for many hungry people. To it we add sand as a prayer for abundance. Sand, whose grains are without number, has in it this essence. What is more plentiful than the sand of Mother Earth in its endlessness? We remember that as we mix our food in its lack of muchness.

"Now, as you knead this dough in your warm hands, bear good thoughts in your heart, that there be no stain of evil in the food. Ask that it may have in it the greatness and power of Mother Earth; then those who eat it will be nourished in spirit as well as in body."

Polingaysi Qoyawayma (Elizabeth White), Hopi

THE WOMAN IS *the planter, the culti-*
vator, the harvester of the corn, and this
[rite] is meant to portray the important
part she plays in the drama of life.

Anonymous, Osage

SHE [YUROK WOMEN] would rise from her bed about four o'clock every morning while the village was yet dark and sleeping, and go to gather wood, praying as she gathered the branches in her basket; and when it was filled she would return to her house, praying all the while, and leave the wood there long before anyone was astir to see her at work. After this task was done, she would go to a high rock on the hillside in a small creek, a short distance from the village, where she would spend the entire day on top of this rock, praying to God and weaving baskets. There was a small basin of water in this solid rock, close by where she sat, which she used to keep her basket materials wet as she worked them. The rock was very high when she sat upon it long ages ago, but it is nearly covered with earth at this present writing. At eventide she would return to her home. So earnest were her prayers, so patient was her humble soul in waiting, that she prayed a number of years on top of this rock, here her prayers were answered in Heaven. Praying in the great solitudes of a vast creation, she never faltered, but prayed on to the Heavenly Father that he might give her strength and courage to become far more pure than any that had ever lived on earth before her, that she might rise as a virgin of purity above her people, leaving in her footsteps the holy halo when she had passed from the earth away to the realms of Heaven above.

Che-na-wah Weitch-ah-wah (Lucy Thompson), Yurok

Unknown
Omaha

COPYRIGHT
1903
BY E.S.CURTIS

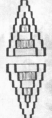

THERE WERE THE long winter moons when the sun never rose above the horizon to lighten the day. But the Eskimos loved this season. There was a magic about the nights that stirred the blood. There were still nights when the Northern Lights swung low across the heavens, and on either side the stars blazed brilliantly in the dark blue sky. On such a night the children played with the Good Shadows, standing silently in a circle, looking up at the flaming golden blanket stretched overhead. "Attai!—Now!" someone would whisper, and then clapping their hands in unison they watched the quiver in the Lights. A whistle too would cause a ripple, but more dramatic were the waves that rolled through the Lights when the deep ice of the lakes or rivers heaved up and cracked apart with thunderous detonations. On calm nights a seal hunter on the coast, or a man fishing at the lakes, might look up and discover by the helpful Good Shadows where the caribou were feeding. Far to the north or south, the east or the west, he had seen a faint rhythmic trembling of the Lights.

On blowy nights the Lights would curl and twist and leap with the wind, and immense ribbons of gold and red would roll and float across the sky. The deeper the winter, the frostier the night, the more brightly glowed the pulsing streamers.

"What makes the Lights?" Anauta would ask.

"Those are Tak-ga-seat, the Good Shadows," Oomialik would answer. "They are put there by the good spirit to help the Inuit. They give us light to see and strength to travel in the long dark winter moons."
To the Eskimos, the Northern Lights proved the existence of a Supreme Power, for they said simply, no man could made the Good Shadows.

Anauta, Inuit

Pretty Medicine Pipe
Apsaroke

I STILL HAVE to explain another phase of Dakota religious life, the quest for a vision. In contrast to that one corporate religious expression, the Sun Dance, all other experience of prayer was private and solitary. It is said by some that originally this was the only way until the custom grew up of joining together in the fulfillment of vows by all those who had pledged themselves during the year. This that I shall describe now is perhaps the oldest, antedating the horse age. Mystics are lonely. Among all peoples they reach out ahead of the masses, and here too that was true. "Lonely is the man with vision." Only certain individuals felt inescapably the call for this effort. By the time a man reached his latter teens he might begin to feel restless and to want some definite influence to guide his future. Such a man decided to fast. So he whispered his idea to some relative, usually a man cousin who himself had gone through a like experience in his youth. The relative helped the novice to prepare. Absolute mastery of physical desires was the prerequisite. The candidate underwent a powerful cleansing through the sweat bath and remained apart after that. Meantime, his "altar," at a place of his own choosing, was prepared for him by his relative.

Then, quietly at some hour unannounced and without fanfare, the young man and his companion slipped away. At the altar, usually on the edge of a remote butte, the man took his place, there to remain all alone on the hallowed plot until someone came to lead him into the <u>Wakan</u> realm. There he hoped to see something supernaturally significant that would help him become a worthwhile man: a good hunter, a good warrior, an effective and true medicine man, a diviner, or whatever. He wanted power to be useful in his tribe. (CONTINUED)

Wife of Old Crow
Northern Cheyenne

He ate and drank nothing; he had only his pipe. After he had fasted a long time, having begun at home of course, his head became light and his senses became so delicate and acute that even a little bit of stick pricking him was unbearably intensified. If a bird called, he might hear a message from the spirit world. If an animal approached him, he might see it as a man to guide him to his vision. Thus he might have the experience of being led by that "man" through the air or over land and sea, resting at last at some spot not to be found on earth where he would receive his revelation. If he heard a song there, he brought it back; if he saw animals or men being restored to life by eating certain herbs, he took careful note of them. In such a case it was his function in life to become a healer and these would be the medicines he would use.

I cannot give any one fasting experience in detail here. They were all very holy, and they were all very involved. They were remembered with photographic clarity, and took a very long while to tell. I have secured several such narratives. They follow the same general pattern, yet in detail they are as varied as human imagination is varied.

A man who had gone through such a spiritual experience would ever after hold in reverence the animal whose spirit led him and would feel a kinship with it. Whenever he was in need of supernatural help he could become <u>en</u> <u>rapport</u> with that spirit and was thereby suddenly enabled to do what was humanly impossible. He was no longer a plain man but one imbued with supernatural strength and power. To get <u>en</u> <u>rapport</u> the visionary sometimes merely thought on his mentor and reached him in that way; at other times he "demonstrated" him by publicly acting out the role of that animal in some characteristic way. While in that role he was mystically identified with it, and through it he derived the superhuman power needed for some special crisis. He thus brought before that mentor of his their spiritual brotherhood and so became re-related to him. As much as to say, "Remember me? I am he to whom you made that promise. Now I need its fulfillment." And such a man earnestly believed he would get that power, and so he did.

This act of reminding a spiritual brother and calling on his help was spoken of as "remembering oneself as bear"—or eagle, or whatever.

Ella Deloria, Yankton Dakota

Wife of Modoc Henry
Klamath

Katie Roubideaux
Brule Lakota

HOW PRETTY THEY are coming.
The rain gods make a sound up above.
How pretty! How pretty! That is so.
That is why this year the rain gods will travel,
How pretty! That is so.
That is why this year the rain will fall,
How pretty! That is so.

Corn-grinding song for the "Sound of the Rain
gods," Isleta Pueblo

I HAVE MADE a footprint, a sacred one.
I have made a footprint, through it the blades push upward.
I have made a footprint, through it the blades radiate.
I have made a footprint, over it the blades float in the wind.
I have made a footprint, over it the ears lean toward one another.
I have made a footprint, over it I bend the stalk to pluck the ears.
I have made a footprint, over it the blossoms lie gray.
I have made a footprint, smoke arises from my house.
I have made a footprint, there is cheer in my house.
I have made a footprint, I live in the light of day.

Planting song (part of women's rite of initiation), Osage

PARENTS ALWAYS IMPRESSED on their children the motto: "Obedi-
ence in listening to the words of wise elders makes a successful medicine person." While the power and the guidance for a career came from
a spirit, it was the elders, learned in these tribal traditions, who provided
the fine points of usage and established the social context for approved
practices.

Grandparents were always kind and indulgent, teaching morality,
through stories and example. They instilled the need for willpower, and
concern for others.

Another warning often repeated with the advice of a tutor emphasized
the importance of the family for an individual. Elders said: "The orphan
has no education, schooling, or advice to become a great person."

Mourning Dove, Salish

ON HIS MIGHTY Throne, high in the infinite realms of Heaven, sat the great ruler of the stars and endless skies, <u>Wah-pee-wah-mow</u> (God). As he peered down through the darkness of a cheerless and lonely space, He created a new world, the earth on which we live. He first made the soil of the earth and placed it in a buckskin sack. He opened the sack and shook the soil from it; it fell down into the chasm of darkness, and <u>Wah-pee-wah-mow</u> could not see anything but the intense darkness. He commanded that the rays of light should penetrate the awful darkness, and there should alternately be night and day, the sun to shine by day and the moon to shine by night, to break the awful stillness of this once dark and cheerless world.

Gazing down from His Throne on high, <u>Wah-pee-wah-mow</u> saw the world he had created was a desolate waste without human life, or life of any kind. He now began the transformation of the new world, and lo, the once barren surface of the earth was clothed in verdure; forests lifted their giant branches skyward; tranquil streams flowed, and great rivers wended their way to the ocean.

The first living thing placed upon the earth was the white deer (<u>Moon-chay-poke</u>). The white deer roamed over the hills, mountains, in the valleys, and on the plains. He was the pride and dignity of the animal kingdom. This is why the Klamath Indians revere the white deer that is so sacred to their hearts and use the skin as an emblem of purity in one of their greatest festivals, or worships, which is termed in English as, "The White Deerskin Dance." In the Indian language it is called <u>Oh-pure-ah-wah</u>, which does not mean dance but means one of their most sacred religious festivals.

The next living creature that <u>Wah-pee-wah-mow</u> placed upon the earth was the red eagle, <u>Hay-wan-alth</u>, who has ever since ruled as the monarch of the skies. The Indians prize the feathers of this eagle very highly, and use them in their great festival. In the decoration of their headgear, they take a single feather, fasten it in the hair at the back of the head, arranging it so that it stands straight up.

<u>Wah-pee-wah-mow</u> did not give our people any single day during the week or month as a day of worship.

When <u>Wah-pee-wah-mow</u> had finished creating the plant and animal life of the earth, He then created the first real man. He made the first man of the soil of the

(CONTINUED)

Unknown
San Carlos Apache

earth, and placed him in the beautiful valley of <u>Cheek-cheek-alth</u>. This valley was located in a far off northern clime. When the first man was created and he became a living being upon the earth, <u>Wah-pee-wah-mow</u> said to him, "You are a living man." God named this man He-quan-neck. Inspired with the breath of life, He-quan-neck first saw the light of day in this sweet valley of sunshine, flowers, fruits, and herbs.

Che-na-wah Weitch-ah-wah (Lucy Thompson), Yurok

WAH-PEE-WAH-MOW IS THE common name, applied to God, used by all classes of our tribe, as the real and true name of God is never spoken. Our high priests, born of the royal marriages, are initiated in the holy lodge and are given the true name of God, but they never speak it outside of the lodge; it is only spoken inside after they have gone through a long and secret communion, and then the name is only whispered in the lowest whisper from mouth to ear. This true name is only used by the priests with profound reverence to the Great Creator in the sacred lodge and in the hallowed lonely places far back on the high mountains where they go to worship in the profound solitudes, away from the gaze of curious people. Our religion has been too sacred, too sublime an ideal to quarrel over; hence we have remained silent through the gloom of so many years and borne patiently the insults on our society as being heathens. This true name of God, as great as the universe, will never be spoken again. If it should be uttered in a loud and harsh tone of voice, it is said that the earth will tremble, ignite in mighty flames, and pass away forever. Ever thus, since the creation of the world, the priests have handed down our religion and traditions from the old land of <u>Cheek-cheek-alth</u>, from generation to generation. It is the duty of every Indian child to be pious and worship the Great Creator. Our sacred religion is <u>Oh-pure-ah-wah</u> (the White Deerskin Dance), where all the members of the tribes [join] in unison and worship, and entertain our guests with much hospitality.

Che-na-wah Weitch-ah-wah (Lucy Thompson),
Yurok

Wife of Mnainak
Yakima

Unknown
Cayuse

RICH IN LIFE, color, and emotion, the Hopi way had been a strong but invisible web, holding the people together. Through their ritual dances, through their songs that had been handed down from generation to generation, they were able to express themselves.

In all things, great and small, the true Hopi saw the forces of creation in operation. This spiritual understanding gave a sense of depth and dignity to their frugal and often difficult everyday existence, as did the unfeigned respect of the young people for the wisdom of their elders, and the devotion of the elders in providing the children with mental and spiritual illumination, as well as physical sustenance.

Polingaysi Qoyawayma (Elizabeth White), Hopi

POLINGAYSI COULD NOT remember a time when she had not made her morning prayer, going with mother, cousins, and aunts to the mesa's edge. First, to rid themselves of evils accumulated during the past twenty-four hours, they would turn and spit over their shoulders; then cleansed and ready to face the new day, they would breath on the corn meal, resting in their hands, and made supplications for long life and good health before releasing the meal into the spirit world by tossing it outward, toward the rising sun.

As the first warming rays of the sun slid over the horizon, touching them with golden fingers, they would reached out, symbolically drawing the beams to them and pressing them to their bodies, meanwhile inhaling deeply and praying that they might be made beautiful in body, face, and heart. Clothed in the armor of all good and all beauty, and protected from evil, they were strengthened to meet the day and its problems.

It would have shocked Polingaysi, as it shocked her parents and other Hopis, had she been old enough to understand that the missionaries considered them wicked and unsaved. Their religion was not a Sunday affair; it was a daily, hourly, constant communion with the Source, the Creator from whom came all things that were, large or small, animate or inanimate, the power behind Cloud People, Rain People, the <u>Kachinas</u> (spirit dancers/people), and all the other forces recognized and respected by the Hopi people. But at that time the little girl mixed religions as confidently as she mixed Hopi parched corn and the Bahana's hard candy.

Polingaysi Qoyawayma (Elizabeth White), Hopi

THE PEACE PIPE was considered such a sacred pact that no one ever broke its laws. If they did, they came to grief brought on by their own untruthfulness, for breaking the law of truth. All that was unclean was never practiced with the peace pipe. The white people, little understanding the power of the pipe as something sacred and holy, doubted the veracity of the peace made with the peace pipe. It is often laughed and jested about by them. The peace pipe, like the white man's sacrament, was a symbol of truth and inward grace; its laws were spiritual and not to be desecrated.

Susan Bordeaux Bettelyoun, Lakota

 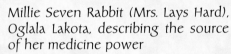 

IT'S NOT ME, it's [the power] from God. That's how I do things.

Millie Seven Rabbit (Mrs. Lays Hard), Oglala Lakota, describing the source of her medicine power

AT ONE TIME there was a young [buffalo] bull. He had four strong legs. As the first three ages passed, he lost three of his legs, one by one. Every year he loses one hair.

The white people are descended from the spider people. They have learned to use electricity. That electricity once belonged only to the Wakinyan [Thunder Beings].

To do this they put up wires on poles. They send these wires all over. As electricity covers the earth, it creates a huge spider web. One day this spider web will cause a great fire. This will cause the buffalo to lose its last leg and fall to the earth. This will be the end of the world.

Little Warrior (Dora Rooks), Oglala Lakota

Wife of Slow Bull
Oglala Lakota

Carries the War Staff
Apsaroke

WHEN MY MOTHER'S sister came to visit, she used to burn cedar, which had green berries. When it was smoking, she would take it into every room to drive away all the evil spirits and keep them away. She always prayed when smoking the room. I use that cedar myself once in a while, even today. It was good and really worked. Today cedar is used in all ceremonies, including the Sun Dance, to drive away evil spirits that might interfere with prayers or harm people.

Agnes Yellowtail Deernose, Absaroke

ONE DAY, AS he sat smoking, I asked him, "Grandfather, who are the gods?" Missouri River took a long pull at his pipe, blew the smoke from his nostrils, and put the stem from his mouth. "Little granddaughter," he answered, "this earth is alive and has a soul or spirit, just as you have a spirit. Other things also have spirits, the sun, clouds, trees, beasts, birds. These spirits are our gods. We pray to them and offer them food, that they may help us when we have need." "Do the spirits eat the food?" I asked. I had seen my grandfather set food before the two skulls of the Big Birds' ceremony.

"No," said my grandfather, "They eat the food's spirit; for the food has a spirit as have all things. When the gods have eaten of its spirit, we often take back the food to eat ourselves."

"How do we know there are gods, grandfather?" I asked.

"They appear to us in our dreams. That is why the medicine man fasts and cuts his flesh with knives. If he fasts long, he will fall in a vision. In this vision the gods will come and talk with him.

"It is not well to provoke the gods. My little granddaughter should never laugh at them nor speak of them lightly."

My grandfather spoke very solemnly.

Waheenee, Hidatsa

IN THOSE DAYS the Sun Dance lasted a long time—a month or more—because they had a lot of societies still active, and a lot of ceremonies to go through. The societies would take turns dancing on different days. There were the Pigeons, Crazy Dogs, Braves, Crow Carriers, and the Horns. The Horns took four days for their dances, and so did the Motokiks, which was made up of women. Then at the end of that they would have a day or two of the Parted Hairs Society—powwow dancing that everybody took part in.

In those days there was a lot of activity with medicine pipes, too. As many as four might be transferred during the time of the Sun Dance. Some of the owners opened their medicine pipe bundles to have a dance and give tobacco out.

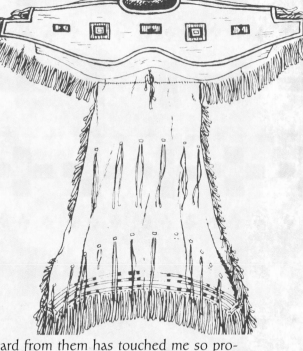

Paula Weasel Head,
Blood

I WISH I could have written the music of the songs. I think they are beautiful. I have heard some of your finest singers, but nothing I ever heard from them has touched me so profoundly as the singing of the Indians. The tears fill my eyes as I listen to their wild, weird singing, and I can never seem to tell myself why.

Among the Omahas, and I suppose in all the tribes, there are men and women, who, though they are not professional storytellers, yet as they can tell stories and legends so much better than any one else, are often

(CONTINUED)

invited by families to come visiting for the sole purpose of storytelling. The best storyteller that I know of in the tribe is Onidabi. Last winter our family took a four days' journey, and with us traveled this man. Evening after evening we gathered round the fire to hear him tell stories, the tent so full that it could not hold another person, and we laughed till the tears came as he told story after story in rapid succession, with such inimitable gestures and changes of tone, that it would have been a study for any of your most accomplished elocutionists, and one by which they might have profited. Any one standing outside the tent and not knowing what was going on within, would have declared that he heard a conversation carried on by several people, when in reality it was only one person speaking, so perfectly did he imitate the tones of old men, women, and children. He did not have to say of his characters, "the old man said this, the young warrior this," or "the little boy said this," but we knew at once by the tone of his voice, who was speaking. When we went to bed at night we would be as tired from laughing as though we had been hard at work all day.

How often I have fallen asleep when a child, with my arms tight around my grandmother's neck, while she told me a story, only I did not fall asleep till the story was finished. When thinking of those old days—so happy and free, when we slept night after night in a tent on the wide trackless prairie, with nothing but the skies above us and the earth beneath, with nothing to make us afraid, not even knowing that there were such beings as white men, happy in our freedom and our love for each other—I often wonder if there is anything in your civilization which will make good to us what we have lost. I sometimes think not. But I am straying from my subject. Thinking of these legends brought back the old days so vividly. I wish I could gather up all the old legends and nursery songs so that they could live after we were dead, but some of them are so fragmentary and nonsensical that I hesitate.

In reading these legends, I hope people will try to imagine themselves in a tent, with the firelight flaming up now and then, throwing weird effects of light and shadow on the eager listening faces, and seeming to sympathize and keep pace with the story, and how we have had only these legends and stories in place of your science and literature.

Bright Eyes (Susette LaFlesche), Omaha

Ho! Ye Sun, Moon, Stars, all ye that move in the heavens,
I bid you hear me!
Into your midst has come a new life.
Consent ye, I implore!
Make its path smooth, that it may reach the brow of the first hill!

Ho! Ye Winds, Clouds, Rain, Mist, all ye that move in the air,
I bid you hear me!
Into your midst has come a new life.
Consent ye, I implore!
Make its path smooth, that it may reach the brow of the second hill!

Ho! Ye Hills, Valleys, Rivers, Lakes, Trees, Grasses, all ye of the earth,
I bid you hear me!
Into your midst has come a new life.
Consent ye, I implore!
Make its path smooth, that it may reach the brow of the third hill!

Ho! Ye Birds, great and small, that fly in the air,
Ho! Ye Animals, great and small, that dwell in the forest,
Ho! Ye Insects that creep among the grasses and burrow in the ground,
I bid you hear me!
Into your midst has come a new life.
Consent ye, I implore!
Make its path smooth, that it may reach the brow of the fourth hill!

Ho! All ye of the heavens, all ye of the air, all ye of the earth;
I bid you all to hear me!
Into your midst has come a new life.
Consent ye, consent ye all, I implore!
Make its path smooth—then shall it travel beyond the four hills!

Song introducing a new child to the cosmos,
Omaha

Unknown
Northern Cheyenne

Index of Quotations

Index of Photographs

Index of Photographers

Anderson, J.A., 76, 136
Barry, D.F., 13, 26, 75
Bell, C.M., 99
Bliss, W.P., 118
Boff, O.S., 41, 116
Choate, John N., 129
Curtis, E.S., 33, 104, 115, 130, 133, 135, 141, 145, 149, 150
DeLancey, Gill, 56, 86
Fiske, Frank, 84, 85
Forsyth, N.A., 68, 89
Gardner, Alexander M., 18, 25
Glacier Studio, 51
Heyn, Herman, 6, 9, 44, 55, 64, 67, 71, 83, 95
Houseworth, Thomas, 47
Huffman, L.A., 3, 34, 38, 153
McClintock, Walter, 37
Randall, A. Frank, 122
Reed, Roland, 1, 121
Rinehart, F.A., 22, 48, 59, 96
Throssel, Richard, 30, 52, 60, 79, 108, 111, 146
Ulke, Henry, 132
Unknown, 4, 10, 15, 16, 20, 21, 29, 42, 62, 63, 72, 80, 87, 90, 93, 101, 102, 103, 107, 112, 125, 126, 137, 142

Biographical Notes

Judith and Michael Fitzgerald have spent extended periods of time visiting traditional cultures and attending sacred ceremonies throughout the world, including the sacred rites of the Apsaroke, Sioux, Cheyenne, Shoshone, Bannock, and Apache tribes. Michael Oren Fitzgerald has written and edited numerous publications on world religions, particularly on American Indian spirituality. He holds a Doctor of Jurisprudence, cum laude, from Indiana University. Michael has taught Religious Traditions of the North American Indians in the Indiana University Continuing Studies Department in Bloomington, Indiana.

Both Michael and Judith have been adopted into the Apsaroke tribe and the family of the late Thomas Yellowtail, one of the most honored American Indian spiritual leaders of the last century. Judith Fitzgerald is a graduate of Indiana University. She is an artisan, calligrapher, and graphic designer, and collaborated with Michael on a series of successful inspirational quote books, including *Indian Spirit* (World Wisdom, 2003). They are married, have an adult son, and live in Bloomington, Indiana.

Dr. Janine Pease is the founding president of the Little Big Horn College in Crow Agency, Montana, a past president of the American Indian Higher Education Consortium, a director of the American Indian College Fund, and a member of the National Advisory Council on Indian Education. She is Vice-President for American Indian Affairs at Rocky Mountain College.

Dr. Pease, a member of the Crow and Hidatsa tribes, has won several prestigious awards: National Indian Educator of the Year, the MacArthur Fellowship "Genius Award," and the ACLU Jeanette Rankin Award. She has been named one of the "One Hundred Montanan's of the Century" by the Missoulian Magazine, a "Montanans to Remember" by Montana Magazine, and one of the fourteen most important American Indian leaders of the twentieth century in *New Warriors*, by R. David Edmunds.

Free American Indian e-Products

Daily Inspirational Quotations

Judith and Michael Fitzgerald have also selected many American Indian inspirational quotations and designed and created many patterns of American Indian e-stationery for use on the Internet. The quotations and e-stationery are combined to create "daily inspirational American Indian quotations" that can be automatically sent to readers each day via e-mail at no charge. Interested readers should visit the e-Products section of the publisher's Internet site at:

<u>www.worldwisdom.com</u>

Other Free e-Products

Judith Fitzgerald has also created American Indian wallpaper, screen savers, e-cards, and e-stationery that are available for no cost at the same website. New products are periodically added. World Wisdom provides all of these products to readers at no cost. The publisher and the editors hope these products will also provide a source of daily inspiration.